Valiant Men Valued Women

∞●∞●∞●∞●∞●∞●∞●∞

A small book of big truths for every man & every woman

Ryan McCoskey

Copyright © 2013 by Ryan C. McCoskey
All Rights Reserved

ISBN: 978-0-9897322-0-8

No part of this publication may be reproduced, stored in a retrieval system, or transmitted, in any form, by any means (electronic, mechanical, photocopying, recording or otherwise), without the prior written permission of the copyright owner. The scanning, uploading, and distribution of this book via the Internet or via any other means without the permission of the copyright owner is illegal.

To my wife, Ashley, who is my sweetest friend, closest companion and life-long lover: You are the most valuable person in my life.

And to my son, Connor, who is growing up in a world in desperate need of valiant men. By God's grace, may he grow up to be one.

Contents

First Things, First

Pride No More: A Preparatory Introduction	3
Truth in Fairytales	11
The Heart of the Matter	19

For your Consideration

Walking in the Light	27
Lead the Life you've been Given	37
Are you Worthy of Imitation?	47

Your Gender Matters, And so do You

Valiant Men & Valued Women	59
The Dance of Marriage	71
You are not what you Feel	87
The Gospel and your Gender	97

As Iron Sharpens Iron
Contributions from Members of The Seed Church

Single, but Never Alone	107
Choose the Harder Thing	117
Your Marriage Needs Community	127
Real Manhood and a Masquerade	135
Multi-Generational Faithfulness	149
Scripture Index	155
Acknowledgements	157

First Things, First

Pride No More:
A Preparatory Introduction

People are like flowers: bright, colorful and mostly unaware. There is such a wide variety of us. Like all the fresh flowers of spring, we live under the illusion that winter will never come for us. Perhaps the comparison of people to flowers is a little too gratuitous; it probably is. If you have any experience of the world whatsoever, you have likely met a few individuals you would not compare to a flower. Maybe a farm animal would be more appropriate.

Before you chuckle too much about that unpleasant person you have in mind, you would do well to remember that no one is better at solving a burglary than a thief. Or, to stick with the farm theme, it usually takes an ass to know one.

In case you weren't paying attention, I just criticized you. I know it's not a very uplifting way to begin a book, but as the old saying goes: "Honesty is the first chapter in the book of wisdom."

This book you are holding is a book of wisdom. Its purpose is to make you more aware of *your* purpose as a man or a woman. That is to say, this book is aimed at helping you comprehend why your gender matters.

But it is more than that. It is also a book about the terrible damage that is caused within a community when men cease to be valiant, and as a result, women are not valued. So you could say this book is twofold in its function. It's intended to expose shortcomings in your life as well as to encourage your healing and growth.

∞●∞●∞●∞●∞●∞●∞

Before we get too ahead of ourselves, it probably makes sense to identify the major hurdle we must overcome before we can make any real progress. We need to talk about everyone's favorite subject: *Sin.*

As I'm sure you know from personal experience, there are all kinds of sin, and thus, all kinds of sinners. There are those who find their comfort in the next strong drink. There are those who live for sex. There are those who trust in money. There are those who find their identity in a career or sex appeal or material possessions. These are examples of how we sin, but there is nothing profound about this kind of sin.

On every street corner you can find someone who cannot control their appetite for something. They have a simple addiction. Not simple as in easy to overcome; simple, as in easy to *understand*. It all begins with a small, secret pleasure. At first, the pleasure is something they can control, but inevitably, it becomes a compulsion that controls them.[1] What was once such a sweet escape becomes a noose around their neck. Addictions can be hidden behind the curtain for a time, but they have a way of always stealing the show.

What all simple addictions have in common is *obviousness*. That is to say, it is rather obvious to everyone that living your life in a drunken stupor is not a good thing. It is also obvious that selling your soul to make a dollar is a bad thing; and even though we might espouse the perpetual playboy in our cinema, we recognize that there are few things more disappointing than a man who would rather burn his honor to the ground than learn how to keep his pants zipped.

The obviousness of these sins is what makes them so simple, and their simplicity affords a measure of protection for society. Everyone knows these things are bad. Any rational person can readily see this, and *that is the point*. If you can see something, then you can identify it; and what can be identified can be avoided. These kinds of sin are often paraded as the really diabolical ones, but they are quite tame compared to the ones we've yet to discuss.

There is a type of sin that is not so obvious. These sins are the *real* monsters. They do not live in your closet or under your bed; no, it's much worse than that. They live in your heart, and if you fail to master them – be assured – they will show no mercy in their enslaving of you.

The worst kinds of sin are those that appear to be *good*. For example, if you were trying to deceive someone, you would be stupid to make up an entirely false story. You would most likely fail in your endeavor to mislead them. But if you adopted a true story, and then proceeded to make a few minor changes – this would probably work. The most effective lie is the one that looks and smells like truth.

In the same way, a sin that can dress itself up as a good work is the most effective sin.[2] These quieter, subtler sins often do the most damage. They are like highly-trained enemy spies operating in secret. They are very hard to identify, and if you fail to root them out, they can single-handedly destroy you. This type of sin has a name. It has been called many things over the ages, but at its birth it was called *Pride*.

At this point, you may be thinking to yourself, 'I don't struggle with the sin of Pride.' Unfortunately for you, this is the most common symptom of the disease. You can be certain you are infected.

Pride is a poison that flows through your veins. It is in you, and it is in me. It persuades you to overlook the flaws in your own character, and at the same time, magnifies those same flaws in others. It beckons you to constantly compare and contrast yourself with others, and assures you that there is always someone worse than you. It encourages you to do 'good' things with totally selfish motives. If truth be told, there is perhaps nothing you have ever done on your own that was truly good – as in truly *selfless*.[3] Even now, it is whispering in your ear, telling you that these words are describing other people, but certainly not you.

Pride is truly a disgusting thing. It's a cowardly thing. It doesn't have the spine to address anyone face-to-face. It just festers in the quietness of your heart. It silently stares and condescends and belittles and undermines. Pride is what made the devil, or should I say, what *un*made him.[4]

This is the hurdle of which I spoke earlier. If you are in the habit of disregarding people who criticize you, then you are not going to care for this book. If you are skilled in explaining away all your faults, then this book is not going to do you any good. Worst of all, if you refuse to accept that you are a prideful person, then you have chosen to make God your enemy. God has a solid track record of opposing the proud, and I do not expect that He will be making any exceptions for you or for me.[5]

Some of you are at a particular disadvantage. You are not only infected with Pride, but also with his even uglier twin brother: *Superficial Religion*. Some of you attend a church or a cathedral or a synagogue or a mosque, and you have a head full of religious teaching, but your life is basically identical to everyone else's. Your religion is just a charade. You keep your religion because it is your chosen method of convincing yourself that you are a good person. And so your religion has become your most despicable sin, by far.

But there is something even worse. There is a type of Pride that trumps all the others. It is the most dangerous and most difficult to detect. It is called *False Piety*, and there is no faster route to hell than this one.

There is a key difference between Superficial Religion and False Piety. A man with a Superficial Religion uses his doctrine to boost his selfish ego, but he does, at least, feel *some sense* of guilt or shame. He goes to church to feel better about himself and is, therefore, going for a selfish motive. But he is at least somewhat aware of his sin. He goes to church because a weekly helping of religion enables him to remain within the illusion that he is a good person.

But those with a False Piety have *no* sense of shame. They are assured of their complete 'rightness', and no one is going to tell them otherwise. These folks are 'good' at religion. They are over-achievers, not because they want to serve and honor others, but because they want to be *served* and *honored* by others. They are playing the devil's part, and playing it rather well. They are always teaching, yet *unteachable*; always 'helping' others to see their problems, yet blind to their own; always careful to point out how much they are needed.

Right now, you are probably thinking of someone who is *just like that*. I hope you were thinking of yourself, but I suspect this isn't so. Unfortunately for you, you've given yourself away once again. No one despises pride in people more than a prideful person.

I suppose you are much worse off than you figured. Hopefully, you are beginning to get comfortable with the fact that you *are* a prideful person. Don't worry, you're in a great company of many not-so-great people – and I'm right there with you.

∞●∞●∞●∞●∞●∞●∞●∞

All of this sobering talk has been for a purpose: to prepare you to read this book. I don't know what you think about the Bible, but I happen to think that it portrays an amazing vision of manhood and womanhood. There is no religion or worldview that champions the courage of a valiant man and the beauty of a valued woman quite like Christianity. I plead with you to open your mind, let go of your opinions for a few hours – surrender your pride – and read this book with a receptive heart.

I previously mentioned that God has a policy of opposing the proud, and He most certainly does. But that's not the whole story. That is only half of it. The other half is that He also has a policy of giving grace to the humble.[6] God is eager to heal and restore those who finally come to the end of themselves.

There is a saying of Jesus that goes a little like this: 'If you try to keep your life, you will lose it. But if you give your life for my sake, you will find it.'[7] In some small way, this summarizes where all of us stand. We can fight to keep a grip on our own sense of goodness, but if we do, we will receive *nothing* from God. If, on the other hand, we choose the more immediately painful option and take full responsibility for all our shortcomings, we will find that our goodness was never worth fighting for in the first place. We will become the recipients of a *real* goodness that actually changes us. Not just at the level of our behavior – but more importantly, at the deepest level, all the way down to the innermost desires of our heart.[8]

On that note, it is time to begin our adventure. Like every good adventure, we must begin with a story.

Once upon a time...

Truth in Fairytales

∞●∞●∞●∞●∞●∞●∞●∞

Once upon a time there was a valiant knight who ate fear for breakfast and danger for dinner (You'll have to forgive me. I'm no good at writing fiction. Just go with it.) This knight was full of courage. He bravely fought nasty and hideous monsters and operated a benevolent not-for-profit in his spare time.

One day, while he was galloping along a forested path on his trusty steed, his eye happened to catch a glimpse of something breathtaking in the distance. Through the trees he could make out the form of a woman brushing her hair. She was at the top of a tower, and her beauty shone down into the forest like the warmth of the sun. As the knight approached the tower, his heart pounded at the sight of this gorgeous woman.

When the knight reached the bottom of the tower, he called up to the mysterious princess. He said, "Good day, young lady. I noticed you from afar and wanted to know if you'd like to go steady with me." She glanced down but offered little enthusiasm. This wasn't her first rodeo. Every knight who noticed her from afar came to the tower, but no man had ever made it to the top.

She said to the knight, "I suppose you would like to come see me in my tower." He playfully replied, "I would love nothing more!" So she threw something down to him, which he caught in the air. It was a scroll. She said, "Within this scroll you will find directions to a cave not far from here. Many men have gone to this cave, but no one has ever come back to the tower. Within the cave there is a great monster you must defeat. If you wish to go steady with me, then you must accept this challenge and return to this tower as the victor." The knight hastily agreed, for he was a brave man.

The directions to the cave were easy enough to follow. He imagined it to be a large, ominous cave, but it was quite ordinary. The opening was barely six feet high, and there was nothing particularly special about this cave, nothing at all. At the mouth of the cavern there was a fire burning in a cauldron and a torch hanging nearby. He lit the torch and began his journey inside.

The air was still. The only sound he could hear was the crackling of the burning torch, softly reverberating off the rock walls. He expected to smell a foul stench; he had defeated many beasts in many caves, and as every knight knows, all the most fearsome monsters smell like sour laundry mixed with rotten Chinese food. It's an awful stench, a manly stench.

But to his surprise, the cave smelled rather pleasant. It had the aroma of vanilla bean and freshly cut strawberries. He wondered what kind of a beast lived in such a sweet-smelling cave. Then, suddenly, he could see something through the glowing light of his torch. He could see.... a sign. He treaded softly and breathed gently, scanning his surroundings with each step, expecting some sort of a trap. But nothing appeared, and he walked right up to the sign.

He held up the torch to read the words upon it. There was a mirror beneath the sign, and he could see his reflection. He caught an image of himself in the mirror and grinned, for he was an exceedingly handsome man. He then proceeded to read the sign.

"Brave knight, you have arrived to the challenge of your lifetime. This is what you must do to go steady with me:

1.) You must sell your steed, retire your armor and get a job. While I do find your gallivanting around to be a little amusing, and somewhat impressive, I need a man who is responsible and reliable. Once we marry, you may go fight monsters on an occasional Saturday, but only after you have taken out the trash and scrubbed the toilet.

2.) You must desire to become a husband first, and a knight second. I know you would like to be widely known and respected for your bravery, but you must die to this desire and choose to honor, nurture and care for me, first. I appreciate that others think you are great. But that matters little to me if you would rather be honored by others than choose to honor me as your wife, your own flesh, your lifelong companion.

3.) You must like the smell of vanilla bean and freshly cut strawberries. It is my favorite perfume. I know you have a brave heart that faces danger, but you must also have a heart that can be tender, sensitive and understanding. I need a man who is courageous and compassionate, strong and sensitive.

4.) Finally, above all, I need a man who loves Jesus more than himself, more than me and more than life. I am not an easy woman to lead. I can be cold and distant, and I need a man who will serve me like Jesus even when I am unlovable. I will grow old and wrinkly, so I need a man who will keep his marriage for nobler reasons than his own pride and pleasure. I want my future children to be courageous and compassionate when they grow up, so they will need a father who can model it for them. Life will get very hard at times, and I need a man who will not buckle under the pressure, one who will bravely suffer like Jesus for the good of his family.

The image you see in the mirror is the challenge of your lifetime. ***You must master yourself.*** *Please return to the tower if you are ready to go steady with me."*

The knight stared into the mirror at his own reflection. The grin was no longer on his face. He left the cave and never returned to the tower, like all those before him. Shortly thereafter, he was savagely eaten by a bear. The end.

∞●∞●∞●∞●∞●∞●∞●∞

It is very likely that you have just read the worst fairytale ever put to paper, but I think it fulfilled its purpose. When the story began you probably had in mind a certain type of ending, didn't you? We can thank the Victorian novelists for that. There is something we love in those old stories. We love the valiant knight. We love the valued princess. Our hearts are captured by the knight who lays down his life for the good of another. Our hearts are stirred by the confident princess who waits for a qualified suitor.

We know these are nothing more than fairytales, but there is something in them we cannot escape. There is a truth in these fairytales, and the truth is quite simple. The truth is *our gender is more than just our anatomy*. There is much more to what makes a man a man and a woman a woman than what meets the eye. There is an undeniable beauty in the interaction between men and women. There is a longing in men to be like the knight and a longing in women to be like the princess.

My fairytale was not so encouraging. It ended rather bleakly, especially for the poor knight. Then again, are we too quickly overlooking the princess? Our knight was savagely eaten, but our princess was left in the tower. Like a vast multitude of women today, the princess was left to face life alone because all the men were too busy gallivanting around.

Like most fairytales, however, our little story was lacking. It was lacking because it only focused on the importance of valiant men and valued women within marriage – but what about men and women in *singleness*? Can a man be single and valiant? Can a woman be single and valued? Of course they can.

This is where our adventure is taking us. We are headed toward comprehending this concept of valiant men and valued women within marriage and with*out* marriage. Men and women do not need marriage to be significant. Some are led to marry, some are not, and that is absolutely satisfactory. But if you are married, then you have a great responsibility. You need to take that responsibility seriously. This book will help you in that endeavor.

On the other hand, if you are single, you may one day be married – but then again, *you may not*. In the event that marriage is not in your future, you must learn to channel your valiance (as a man) or value (as a woman) in other ways. Single people are not any less significant than married people; they have a particular role to play. You *can be* a valiant single man or a valued single woman.

∞●∞●∞●∞●∞●∞●∞●∞

For a moment, allow me to briefly talk about the princess's fourth requirement. She required that her suitor must love Jesus more than himself, more than her and more than life. Why does this matter?

Loving Jesus matters because Jesus had a very particular way of living his life. Jesus insisted that living an abundant life consisted not in submitting to our passions, but in *mastering* them. According to Jesus, people could not really live without denying themselves and following him.[1] People who authentically love Jesus desire to live like him, and to live *for* him, not because they are seeking to please themselves, but to please Jesus.

Perhaps this sounds a little silly to you, but that's only because you don't understand the degree of your heart's deception. Do you understand what it means to master your passions? This is no small task. This is a lifelong pursuit. Without the love of Jesus in your heart, mind, and soul, you will not be successful. Loving Jesus is a *prerequisite* for gaining control of your heart. There are a variety of ways to adjust your behavior for a season, but only Jesus can bring real, lasting change.[2]

Now, for a moment, allow me to address those of you who are very skeptical of my words because you know people who say they love Jesus, and yet they are not 'changed' people.

First off, you could just be a graceless person. Knowing Jesus does not mean you become the sinless savior of the world. It doesn't work like that. It's a long, hard process with many failures along the way. It could be that, in your heart, you are constantly waiting for 'redeemed' people to fail because you have some personal reservations about Jesus and the whole Christianity thing. If that's where you are, then you have only further proven my point: that, without Jesus, you are a vindictive, graceless person who is mastered by foul passions.

It is very possible, however, that you *do* know some people who are quite like our knight. They enjoy suiting up in their armor, galloping on a steed and proving their salt with a monster or two. But in the end, they are just posers. When it comes to the real work, they run because they don't really follow Jesus. There are many people like this, but honestly, why does that matter to you? Do you think that parenthood should be thrown out because you've witnessed a few bad parents? Have you burned all your money because some have misused theirs? It should not be too surprising that there are fake Christians, and it is not logical to assume that all of Christianity is phony merely because some alleged followers are.[3]

∞●∞●∞●∞●∞●∞●∞●∞

In the coming chapters we are going to spend our time discussing what valiant men and valued women look like, and how their exemplary lives make much of Jesus and other people. But we would be remiss to go straight there. We need to take the scenic route.

The truth is that *no one* starts their journey well. We all have a past.[4] You may be a valiant man or a valued woman today, but you weren't always a good example for others. Perhaps some of you are terrible examples *even now*. If you are, then rest at ease. I would like to be an encouragement to you. You need to understand that loving Jesus and other people does not start with you – *it starts with Jesus*. We learn how to love Jesus and others by fully experiencing Jesus' love for us.[5]

What does it mean to fully experience the love of Jesus? Maybe that sounds like a warm and fuzzy thing, but it's quite the opposite. Experiencing Jesus' love is very hard, at first. It is hard because the first place we must go is precisely the place we do not want to visit, at all. And yet this place is where Jesus' grace is felt most. We must go to this place because Jesus will not meet us anywhere else. We must either meet him here or never meet him.

To be valiant men and valued women we have to walk in the light. The problem is we cannot walk in the light until we are ready to expose what is hiding in the dark. *This is the hard part.* But if you refuse to do it, then you will never know Jesus. This is where you first meet him: In the dark, dingy basement of your soul, where you have stored all the things you'd rather not think about, ever again. This is where he will meet you, and this is where you will learn a lesson you'll never outgrow. The lesson is simple: Grace changes everything.

As for what exactly this looks like – we'll be getting to that soon enough.

The Heart of the Matter

Walking through a shopping mall is an interesting experience these days – rather enlightening, in fact. The storefronts are plastered with posters and ads and banners. Muscular mannequins wear the latest fashions. Everywhere you look, you can find someone selling some version of manhood or womanhood.

There is such a wide variety of options. If you want to dress like a casual surfer dude, there's a store for you. If you want to look like a Gucci model, there's a store for you. If you want to wear shirts that seem two sizes too small, there's a store for you. Everyone is selling a version of men, and everyone is selling a version of women.

What I find amusing is how little any of it has to do with being a man or a woman. It would seem that looking a certain way and wearing a certain fashion has become the primary marker of gender identity in our culture. Men desperately want to be valiant, so they join overpriced gyms, take overpriced supplements and wear overpriced clothing. The fitness and apparel companies have convinced us that manhood is all about how we look.

It's no different for women, except it's probably *worse*. Women desperately want to be valued, and there's a standard protocol for that as well. You have to appear younger than you really are, wear clothing that makes you look thinner than you really are, and whether or not you are succeeding has everything to do with how often boyish men stare and grope at you.

I think it's safe to say our culture is a parody of gender identity. Men desire to be men, but most men haven't the slightest clue what real manhood looks like. Women desire to be women, but most women are stuck in the same rut. And this is because we're always going about it the wrong way.

We can be sure of at least one thing: What we're doing isn't working. Not only is it not working, but it's making things worse. Our vision for what men and women *should be* has become anemic. We're far too easy to please. We've settled for fashion and fitness and face creams, and as a result, these have become the primary markers of gender identity in our culture.

We need to start at the root. We need to change our definition of valiant men and valued women. We need to take seriously our responsibility to leave a strong legacy for all those who are watching us and learning. And we need all the help we can get for such an ambitious endeavor.

∞●∞●∞●∞●∞●∞●∞

First, we need to define valiant men before we can define valued women. We must do so in this order because this is how men and women were designed. Valiant men make for valued women, and in the same way, selfish men make for women who have to fend for themselves and their value.

Now this is *not* to say that women need men *in order* to be valuable. That's not the case at all. Women are inherently valuable. But history has shown that bad men tend to ruin the women around them. They use them and abuse them. Rather than helping them to flourish, they cause them to wither. Bad husbands and bad fathers are like a cancer to cultures.

If we are going to talk about valiant men, then we have to talk about responsibility. Real manhood is all about *responsibility*.[1] Men are designed to bear burdens, not in the weight room, but in the real world for the good of others. Men are supposed to be reliable. Men are supposed to be trustworthy. Men are supposed to be courageous.

But responsibility is more than just getting things done. Responsibility is not just keeping your job, and paying your bills, and mowing your lawn. Responsibility includes seeing to the needs of those in your care. Responsible men are courageous, and also *compassionate*. Sometimes men must be strong; at other times they must be sensitive.

All men have this built-in desire to be strong, but it's usually channeled in childish ways. Our culture thinks about strong men as guys who can bench a lot of weight, but that's the most *meaningless* type of strength. A strong man works 50 hours a week to make ends meet for his family. A strong man has control over his temper. A strong man makes a commitment and keeps it. A strong man reads bedtime stories to his kids, and takes out the trash, and builds an intimate friendship with his wife.

Valiant men, regardless of their marital status, are responsible – with their time, their talents and their treasure. They don't live for themselves; they live for others. They care about their community. They are disciplined. They honor the women in their midst, and they challenge other men to grow up and become valiant.[2]

Men who think about manhood this way are easy to follow because *they are leaders*. They're not good at leading because they have the latest leadership book or because they are tall enough to stand out in a crowd; they're good at leading because of what they're not: self-centered. They have made a decision to bear burdens for others rather than create more burdens for society.

∞●∞●∞●∞●∞●∞●∞

It's not too difficult to see how valiant men make for valued women. When men are responsible, the women in their midst flourish. Valiant men help women readily sense their value. Women who are surrounded by good men know they don't need boob jobs or liposuction to be beautiful. Women don't have to pretend like they're younger or thinner when they're loved by valiant men (though sometimes they still choose to).

Valued women are secure in their identity. Not conceited and snooty, but secure. Valued women don't have to *pretend* to be secure – they *are* secure. They know who they are. They don't have to spend all their time posturing in the mirror of public opinion.

Valued women draw the best out of men. They have a kind of beauty that transcends physical appearance.[3] They don't swoon for boyish men or itch to show themselves off.

Valued women don't settle for lackluster displays of manhood.

This kind of woman is hard to find in the absence of good men. This is not to say that it *never* happens. But bad men are like millstones – when they run from responsibility and sink into selfishness, they drag others down with them. When men act like boys, they don't value women well, and this can cause women to look for their value in unhealthy places. Precious daughters with piss-poor dads often find themselves with rotten men – not because they want to be mistreated, but because they've never experienced better. It's hard to look for something you don't know exists.

A woman doesn't need a husband in order to *be* valuable; she doesn't need a man to validate her. But when a man lays down his life to help a woman flourish, it makes a serious impact on her. Whether single or married, valiant men make for valued women who are secure in their identity.

Men should be cognizant of how the women in their midst are being valued. Reminding a woman of her value usually has very little to do with poetic love letters or sappy displays of emotion. On the contrary, it's much more likely a woman will sense her value if men will be consistently reliable for her, honest with her, gentle in demeanor, and intent on serving before being served. The grandiose displays have their place, but they cannot compensate for a lack of consistent, simple acts of service.

Any man can plan something special in order to make a woman sense her value, but few men are attentive to all the daily small things, which are, to be sure, not of small importance at all. Men who have a habit of dreaming up ideas about how they *could* accomplish something great should spend less time dreaming about things that are not and spend more time paying attention to things that are. Holding open the door, carrying the larger suitcase, taking out the trash, and washing the dishes speak a better word than majestic intentions.

∞•∞•∞•∞•∞•∞•∞

    There is much more to be said about what makes men valiant and women valued. If you are feeling any objections welling up inside of you, then just keep reading. Perhaps I will address your objection in the following pages.

    What I want you to grasp right now is the heart of the matter, and the heart of the matter is this: Our world is in *desperate* need of valiant men and valued women.[4] Our families need them, our communities need them, our churches need them, our businesses need them, our children need them, our government needs them – *our world desperately needs valiant men and valued women.*

∞●∞●∞●∞●∞●∞●∞

For your Consideration

∞●∞●∞●∞●∞●∞●∞

Walking in the Light

∞•∞•∞•∞•∞•∞•∞•∞

    I think our society is not too intrigued by Christianity, as long as it works in a manner similar to other religions and worldviews. A Christianity that causes people to become political is expected. A Christianity that makes people moralistic is understandable. A Christianity that encourages its followers to join a sub-culture filled with 'Christian' music, apparel, catch-phrases, bumper stickers and books is tolerable. All of this is quite ordinary – except, of course, the kind of Christianity that actually produces authentic Christians.

    A fairly recent (and unfortunate) development in the English language has been the rise of overusing the word 'Christian' as an adjective. Any item can now be a 'Christian' item. That is to say, a trinket can be transformed into a 'Christian' trinket by stamping a Bible verse upon it. Some radio stations play music, but others play 'Christian' music. The difference is rather simple: As long as you incorporate a lyric about forgiveness or prayer or some other vague concept of loving-kindness, then you may safely call it a 'Christian' song.

This seems silly to me. It seems silly because it promotes a kind of Christianity that has very little good to offer society. A 'Christian' shirt, for example, is just a shirt. It is like every other shirt, except that it bears some trite saying upon it about Christianity. It only gives lip service to the faith, and that's what makes it a 'Christian' shirt.

In like manner, I am afraid there are many more 'Christian' people than there are Christians. A 'Christian' person is like a 'Christian' shirt. They have adopted a kind of Christianity that makes them political or moralistic or part of a sub-culture, but overall, they are quite like any other person. They point to the Christian faith, but only superficially. A Christian, however, is something entirely different.

A Christian, by definition, is someone who embodies the ministry of Jesus. I do not mean they die on a cross for the sins of the world; a Christian does not *become* Jesus, they only embody or live in accordance with his ministry. What this means is that *a Christian is someone who incorporates a Biblical worldview into the real world.*[1]

A 'Christian' man, for example, goes to church. He intellectually agrees with the tenets of Christianity. He stands for moral goodness. He believes in God, and even Jesus. But for the most part, his Christianity is more like a pair of gloves than a full wardrobe. A 'Christian' man's Christianity is only a small compartment within his life. It is mostly moralistic. It sits in the mind, and has never traveled to the heart. A 'Christian' man is like a 'Christian' shirt: he mostly looks and acts like any other man.

The Christian man, on the other hand, incorporates a Biblical worldview into his family time, his work, his relationships and his hobbies. He embodies the ministry of Jesus. Instead of living within a sub-culture, he engages the real world with the message of the Gospel. His Christianity has permeated him. Like the 'Christian' man, he agrees with the tenets of Christianity, but unlike the 'Christian' man, it's an affair of his head, his heart and his hands.[2]

All of this is important to our discussion of valiant men and valued women for a simple reason: *A Christianity that cannot transform us is of no use*, and in fact, is not really Christianity at all. What good is a religion that changes how you vote on social issues, but has no affect upon your compassion and patience for others? There is no use in talking about being a valiant man or a valued woman if it's all talk that only leads to more useless talk.

Before we go much further, we should take some time to establish the difference between the 'Christian' person and the Christian. We have discussed how they live differently, but what exactly causes this difference? If you were to boil down the essence of these two people, what would you get?

Entire books have been written in an attempt to explain how someone makes the transition to becoming a Christian. If you are looking for a more thorough treatment of this subject, do not look to me. This is not the place, nor am I even qualified to lead such a discussion. I can only give you a sense of it.

The primary difference between the 'Christian' person and the Christian is this: *The Christian walks in the light*. If you are unfamiliar with the New Testament, particularly of John's writings, then this probably means very little to you – but stay focused with me; you will soon see the significance. At this point, it would serve you well to read 1 John 1:5-10. Unless you have put it to memory, you need to turn there and read it now. I'll even provide a short intermission for you to do so.

∞•∞•∞•∞•∞•∞•∞

Some of you moved immediately to this text without first referencing the Scripture I politely asked you to read (tsk-tsk). You will not fully understand what I'm going to tell you if you are unfamiliar with this passage. Don't worry, I'll provide an opportunity for you to right your wrong. Go ahead and read 1 John 1:5-10, and I will meet you here once you've finished.

∞•∞•∞•∞•∞•∞•∞

In this brief passage we are given a compelling word-picture that serves to illustrate the difference between the 'Christian' person and the Christian. It is immediately clear that regardless of what we *say* about our knowledge of God and our love for others, we don't really know Him or practice love if we do not walk in the light. So how exactly do we walk in the light?

In order to answer this question we have to get a little uncomfortable. We need to take a short walk down the stairs of your heart into the dark, dingy basement where you store all the baggage you've intentionally hidden from others. This is where walking in the light first begins.

If you are anything like me (and I suspect you are), then you are not too excited about this. You are saying to yourself "sure, sure, let's go down there," but you have no intention of walking down those stairs – and I'm right there with you. Personally, I am ashamed of my basement. I am ashamed because I feel that if someone *really* knew who I was and exactly what I was capable of, then they could not possibly love me, much less *like* me. Surely, nothing good can come from rummaging through all that baggage.

∞●∞●∞●∞●∞●∞●∞●∞

    All of us tend to do two things with the basement baggage in our hearts. First, we hide it. We pretend like it's not there. We hide from God and others because we reason that we could never be truly and fully loved if we were exposed. We make ourselves out to be something we are not by keeping parts of our life in the dark.
    The second thing we do is rename some of the baggage, pull it upstairs, and use it to furnish our heart. We call our selfish ambition 'motivation' and show it off. We refer to our crippling anxiety as 'carefulness.' We call our sexual perversion 'love' or 'chemistry' or 'a harmless preference.' We prize our empty, legalistic religion as a 'strong moral compass.' We pass off our chronic laziness as 'waiting on the Lord.'
    When we walk in the dark, we hide, either by pretending we have no baggage or by justifying our baggage and acting as though it isn't a problem. Essentially, when we walk in the dark we don't have any *real* fellowship with *anyone*. Our relationships with other people are surface-level and phony because we are guarded; likewise, our relationship with God is phony because we are pretending like He can't see through our silly justifications. When we walk in the dark, we isolate ourselves.
    You can remain in the dark and be a 'Christian' person, but you will never become a Christian that way. You

Valiant Men. Valued Women.

can listen to the radio stations, wear the shirts, attend all the best conferences, talk the lingo and read the books – but none of those 'Christian' things will make you a Christian. You cannot embody the ministry of Jesus if you will not go where he is. Try all you want, but you will not find Jesus in the dark. He is in the light because *he is pure light*.

It is right here, at this point, where we are prone to get it wrong. This is where we assume that if Jesus went into our basement, he would probably beat us to death. We can almost see God shaking his head in disappointment, wondering when we're going to get it together. We can feel his scorn. How could he love us, much less like us in view of all this dreadful baggage?

This, my friend, is why you need the sweet scandal of the *Gospel*. This is where grace changes everything. According to the Bible, God has already punished someone for your baggage. He already beat someone to death for it. This was the whole point of the cross. The reason why we can step into the light without fearing God is because our baggage has already been dealt with.[3]

Now this sounds a little far-fetched, doesn't it? After all, your baggage is still there! Some of it you are hiding; some of it you have proudly hung on the walls of your heart, pretending like it's not a problem. How is it possible that God has dealt with your baggage when it's still there? Let me tell you more about the Gospel and why we must walk in the light.

Walking in the light is not something we do because we have nothing to hide. *All of us have plenty to hide*. We walk in the light because Jesus has already been in our basement, and he still desires to know us. We do not walk in the light *after* our baggage is gone. That will never happen. Instead, we confidently walk into the light, dragging our baggage with us, because Jesus is a gracious God who has promised to heal us.

This is only possible because of Jesus' death. Without the work of Jesus on the cross, walking in the light would be a *terrible* thing. Exposing ourselves would mean alienation from God and others. But within the grace of Jesus, walking in the light brings healing. As we walk in the light, Jesus deals with our baggage, in real time. The punishment for the baggage was dealt with on the cross – now the baggage itself is dealt with, day by day, as we walk with him and others in honesty and humility.[4]

This is what separates the Christian from the 'Christian' person. As a Christian, your whole life is accountable before God: Your marriage or singleness, your children, your friendships, your work ethic, your self-control, your care for your body, your self-image, your addictions, your patience, your endurance; we could go on and on. *A Christian walks in the light.* It's not an event that once happened or something that will happen; it's something that happens *repeatedly* with God and others.

∞•∞•∞•∞•∞•∞•∞

This process of walking in the light must be the engine of our motivation. When we move toward Jesus into the light, our baggage is exposed. Regardless of your maturity, you will *always* have baggage, and you will always have to carry it into the light to remain in fellowship with God and others. This may sound awful, but because of the Gospel, it's one of the sweetest aspects of the Christian life.

When we expose our baggage to God and others, it reminds us that we're not that impressive. The pressure of performing to gain acceptance melts away. Instead of receiving condemnation, Jesus warmly invites us into his presence and freely cleanses us from all our sin. The sweet scandal of the Gospel is that your baggage, *as real as it is*, has no power over you when you walk in the light with Jesus.[5] It's in your basement, it's hanging on the walls of your heart, and it needs to be dealt with – but it's *powerless* to condemn you because of Jesus' death and resurrection. This is the engine of the Christian life.

∞●∞●∞●∞●∞●∞●∞●∞

You may think we've taken a useless detour on our journey together, but we haven't. It's crucial that you get this. We cannot move on to talking about valiant men and valued women until this has become clear to you: You will *never* become the man or woman you must become until you start walking in the light with God and others.

If your motivation to become valiant or valued is propelled by the grace of Jesus who can deal with your baggage, then you have an engine that will not burn out. But if your motivation is self-centered and rooted in pride, then you are walking in darkness. You will not become the man or woman you must be. You will hide in your basement and continue to pretend like your baggage is not a problem. Your heart will not change, and you will burn out. The self-help books and positive thinking mumbo-jumbo will adjust your behavior for a time, but you won't really change. Not until you walk in the light.

Now would be a good time to ask yourself whether or not you are in any condition to read on. Perhaps you need to step away for a bit and evaluate whether you are living like the Christian or the 'Christian' person. Do you embody the ministry of Jesus in your life or are you more like the

'Christian' shirt, giving lip service to Godly values, yet living like every other person who walks in the dark?

If you are hiding in your basement, working so hard to keep all that baggage hidden, then it's time to turn on the light. It's time to expose yourself. Perhaps there is some baggage upstairs you're playing off as something good. It's time to call it for what it is and quit playing games.[6]

Are you afraid to step out of the dark? I understand your fear because it scared me, too. But hear me out: *Jesus is not going to reject you*. He will cleanse you, and you will be free.[7] Face the consequences; do what's right; walk in the light and restore authentic fellowship with God and others in your life.

Now let's get on with it.

Lead the Life you've been Given

There is perhaps nothing more common to human experience than the feeling of *discontentment*. This nagging ache we call discontentment has been described in innumerable ways. All of us have experienced it, and we have said things that exposed our feeling of it. Some of us have spoken phrases like, "I'm just not happy anymore," or "why can't things be different?" Maybe you can recall thinking things like, "if only such and such was more enjoyable, then everything would be better," or "if only Mr. So and So would change, then I'd be fine."

To be fair, these sentiments are not always bad. At times, discontentment can lead to positive change. But more often than not, we say these kinds of things to convince ourselves that the grass is greener on the other side – even when we know better. We become discontented very easily, and when that nagging ache appears, the first line of defense is to pretend like we are a helpless victim of our situation. In those selfish moments, we cling to the illusory idea that our problems have nothing to do with us, and if only everyone else and everything else would change – why then, life would be pleasantly livable.

For the vast majority of us, these feelings are not only untrue, but also totally *unreasonable*. It is exceedingly rare that anyone gets anywhere in life without being intimately involved. People have influenced us and circumstances have changed us, but that doesn't mean we are empty vessels, guided purely by outside forces. Whether or not we care to admit it, most of us stand where we are because we made a set of decisions that resulted in our current life situation.

What I'm about to say is very plain and obvious; although I am saying it at the risk of appearing dull, I still think it needs to be said: *The life you currently have is your life*. This is, quite simply, how reality works. Your life is not defined by what you *used* to be; your life is not defined by what you *want* to be; your life is what it is, at this very moment.

If you are a married man, then you are no longer single. Although you may *want* to be a good husband, if you are not seeking to courageously and compassionately serve and lead your wife, then you simply aren't a good husband. You are not what you once were, nor are you what you want to be – *you are what you are*, right now, as you read this sentence.

Before you begin to feel too hopeless, please understand that I am not endorsing fatalism. I'm not trying to make you feel like a lost cause. Instead, I am trying to help you recognize that you are responsible for your life. According to the Bible, you will give an account for how you live it, and the One who will demand your account is the One who provided you with your life in the first place.[1]

Yes, I am talking about God. He has given you your life, and He has made you responsible for it. It is not yours to keep (at least, not yet), but only yours to borrow for the time being. There will come a point in time when your body no longer functions due to old age, disease or injury, and you will die. It is then that you will be required to give your account, and it is then when God will decide whether you get to keep your life or lose it.

∞•∞•∞•∞•∞•∞•∞•∞

Sometime around year 55 AD, a Jewish man named Paul wrote a letter to a group of Christians in the city of Corinth. In this letter, aptly titled "1 Corinthians" in the Bible, Paul encouraged the Corinthian Christians to *lead the life they had been given*.[2] This instruction from Paul may appear rather simple, but the implications of this teaching are quite profound.

Paul wrote these words because he wanted the Corinthians to understand that Christianity is relevant to all people, in all kinds of life circumstances. Some of the Christians in Corinth were raised in devout Jewish families. Some of them did not understand Judaism very well at all. Some came from affluent families, while others were bondservants. There were married folks and single folks, young adults, as well as more seasoned individuals. The church at Corinth was made up of all kinds of people in various life situations.

It's interesting to note what Paul did *not* say. He did not say, "If you want to be a useful person, then you must get married," nor did he say, "Stay single if you want to honor God." Paul did not tell those with a Jewish background to pretend like they were never Jews, nor did he instruct individuals who were raised outside of Judaism to suddenly start acting like Jews. Paul did not prescribe a certain life situation that everyone had to accept in order to honor God.[3] Instead, he simply told them to lead the life they had been given.

We should not overlook the significance of this instruction, especially as it relates to our addiction to discontentment. There is, I think, a tendency in all of us to waste an *untold* amount of time and energy trying to figure out the next step in life, rather than considering how we can honor Jesus with our life, as it stands.

Our culture is full of singles who dream about getting married, as well as married people who lament the loss of their singleness; the former are convinced that a spouse will make all things right, while the latter are convinced that their spouse is all things wrong. Rather than leading the life they have, they surrender to their discontentment and are led astray.

Our infatuation with wanting to be somewhere else in life is rather ironic. Youngsters daydream about the freedom they will have once they grow older, while older folks daydream about the freedom they enjoyed as youngsters. It seems we are experts at convincing ourselves that the future or the past is always superior to the present. The life we have withers away as we burn our best years dreaming about what will be or lamenting what once was. This is why we must lead the life we've been given: The alternatives are futile.

Paul's instruction to the Corinthians is supremely relevant to our discussion of valiant men and valued women. In our culture there is nothing that makes a person discontent quite like singleness, except, of course, marriage. What a stupid paradox it is! Single people can't wait to get married, and married people can't wait to get away from their spouse. The Bible has a word for this. It's called *idolatry*.

Idolatry is simply the act of making natural things divine things. Singleness and marriage are divinely created things by a divine Creator, but they are *not* divinities. You can use them for divine reasons, and you can redeem them to be beautiful, God-glorifying things, but in and of themselves, singleness and marriage are not gods worthy of your devotion. Marriage should *never* be considered a savior from singlehood, nor should singlehood be considered a savior from marriage. If you make these things more than they are, then you will make your life much less satisfying. You will spend all your days grasping at shadows.

∞●∞●∞●∞●∞●∞●∞●∞

I don't know if you've caught on to this quite yet, but there is an important principle of Christianity behind all of this. The principle is that God's power to satisfy your soul is bigger than your place in life.[4] God is sovereign. This means that people within marriage, as well as people without marriage are equally within God's divine plan. You don't have to conform to man-made traditions to find fulfillment because *God made man*. His principles are infinitely superior.[5]

There are many cultures in the world that do not see the value of single women. Perhaps many in America feel this way, too. The apostle Paul would suffer none of that garbage. Women need not be married to live meaningful lives full of God's grace, and that goes for men, as well. The idea that marriage enhances the value of a person is preposterous. Marriage is most certainly a divine creation of God – but so is *singleness*.

To lead the life we've been given means to be intimately engaged in our life, as it stands. Rather than wishing we were someone or somewhere else, we are encouraged to honor Jesus with what we have today. We are warned about the dangers of living in continual discontentment.

On a practical level, there are all kinds of ways to apply this teaching, and Paul helps us to apply it effectively. Within his letter, he told the Corinthians to remember that they were purchased by God, and therefore, that they should not become slaves to men.[6] Paul wanted them (and us) to see that God saves people for a purpose. Jesus endured the suffering of the cross so we could be reconciled to God, and that reconciliation is *purposeful*. There was a purpose in it, and there is a purpose for it.

The problem is we often overlook God's grace in saving us, and as a result, we go back to living under the expectations of other people, rather than living according to the wisdom and grace of God. It is like being redeemed from slavery, only to return to your captor. It is like being set aside for an honored purpose, only to abandon it for a lowly one.[7]

If Jesus has beckoned you to walk in the light, and if you have tasted his grace for your sin, then you have an honored purpose in his plan. You have been purchased from the debt of your sin by the blood of Jesus. This means you have been redeemed from the worldly expectations of people and set aside for the purposes of God.

As for what this looks like, you need not look very far. Are you a single guy right now? Then lead the life you've been given, honor Jesus with your singleness, and if God gives you a healthy passion for a valued woman, then pursue her. Perhaps God will lead you to a spouse, *and perhaps not*. Either way, your identity should not be staked on that purpose. Remember: You're not a slave to worldly principles anymore, so don't make marriage your savior.

What if you are a married man? Then lead the life you've been given, honor Jesus with your marriage, and love your wife with the graceful love of Jesus. Be where you are, serve where you are, and lead where you are. Instead of spending energy daydreaming about the simplicity of your long-past singlehood, invest in your wife today. Be a valiant man so your wife can be a valued woman.

The exact same can be said for women. Whether in singleness or in marriage, lead the life you have now. Don't stake your identity on how men judge your beauty or worth because you've been freed from that. If you're a single woman, then you don't need a husband to give you value anymore than a diamond needs a ring to be valuable. If you're a married woman, then you have a husband and singleness is not your place in life, so don't idolize being single. Lead the life you've been given.

Now let me be clear. Do not allow this brief chapter in this small book to be your exhaustive understanding of what it means to lead the life you've been given. You need to read the entire letter of 1 Corinthians, and especially chapter seven. Paul has much to teach you, and you would be very wise to understand his words as best you can, not only because Paul was wise, but more importantly because God was behind every word that Paul penned in that letter. As you learn from Paul, you will learn from God, not because Paul spoke for God, but because God spoke *through* Paul.

There is much more to say in our discussion of valiant men and valued women in marriage and singleness, and how our gender has great purpose, but for now, soak up this principle: *Lead the life you've been given*. Quit surrendering to your discontentment.[8] Quit running from the present. Don't burn up your best years wishing you were someone or somewhere else. Take responsibility for the life you have because you will give an account for it.

∞•∞•∞•∞•∞•∞•∞•∞

    It is profitable to look forward to the future because it fills us with the hope of heaven and the joy of knowing God truly *and* fully. It is also profitable to consider the past, as it teaches us much about life. But refuse to become a slave to your carnal discontentment. If you submit to that yoke of slavery, then your life will be filled with meaningless waste as you grasp for future things that may never be and wish for past things that once were.

    Leading the life you've been given is much more difficult than running from the present, but it's also much more *rewarding*. Many of us will grow old enough to find out what it feels like to have a past that dwarfs our future. At that time we may realize what a terrible mistake we've made. Our habit of wasting year after year dreaming about the future and longing for the past will leave us with a bank of memories we'd rather forget and a miniscule future with little hope.

    If you run from the present now by living for the future and longing for the past, then a time will come when your past and your future will *abhor* you. Then, for the first time, you will be forced to live in the present because you will be ashamed of how little your past mattered, and you will be afraid of what little future you have left.

Put your discontentment to death, recognize that God has an honored purpose for you, and lead the life you've been given.

Are you Worthy of Imitation?

∞●∞●∞●∞●∞●∞●∞●∞

    I have grown weary of the term 'role model.' It has become such a hum-drum, lifeless idea because we've drained the meaning from it. We have overused it, and even worse, used it for *stupid* purposes.

    In some ways, it seems as though the modern notion of the 'role model' has become the golden ticket of escape for every parent who would rather live like a child than raise children. If you want your kids to do what you say (heaven forbid they do what you do), then draw their attention to a 'role model.' As long as we can trust athletes or business moguls or performers to guide our children, then we are free to go about our business without the hindrance of having to model anything for anyone.

    Think with me, for a moment, on the irony of the modern 'role model.' Imagine a father sitting at home, bossing his family around, living for his own comfort, shutting down emotionally after a day of work, harboring bitter resentment toward the 'burden' of his family and, of course, watching the television. Imagine his young son watching it with him. (Cue the commercial break) – and there he is: The modern 'role model.' An athlete appears and talks about the importance of working hard and serving others. Fantastic. The young boy takes an interest in the athlete and wants to be like him. The parents take notice, so they buy jerseys and shoes and posters for their son.

Now I have no qualms with jerseys or shoes or posters, but what I do find disturbing is that a man who the boy has never met is making a bigger impact upon his life than the man who has been given the primary responsibility of modeling manhood for him. I wish I could make some sort of whimsical joke about it, but it only makes me feel a deep sense of sadness. *What a tragedy.*

I fear that it may be even *worse* for young girls. The world of entertainment often looks like a land of freedom, but it is actually a hell-hole ruled by the ignorant expectations of people and enslaved to the power of the dollar bill. If you want to stay in fashion, then you need merchandise. But, of course, your merchandise won't sell unless it appeals to the masses. For a young female star, there is no better way to drive sales than to become the next round of eye candy for pubescent boys. What a fine legacy to leave with young girls. What a helpful life lesson.

At this point, it would be very easy for us to spend more time criticizing celebrities, and to conclude that *they* are the real problem. But that would be just another avoidance tactic. It's not enough to let a 'role model' lead your child, but it's also not enough to sit around and whine about the stupidity of celebrities. If you're a parent, then you need to lead. You need to invest in your kids. You need to sacrifice. You need to be *worthy of imitation.*

Are you Worthy of Imitation?

∞ • ∞ • ∞ • ∞ • ∞ • ∞ • ∞ • ∞

I am rather fond of the phrase 'worthy of imitation.' It sums up so much in so few words. I didn't come up with it, though. It's in the Bible. In the New Testament there is a letter titled "Hebrews," and within it we are encouraged to observe the lives of good leaders and to imitate them.[1] If we want to live noble lives, then we need to reflect on the Godly leadership of all those who have gone before us and learn from their worthy examples.

The implication of this teaching should be quite clear, but let me put it within the context of this book. If we desire to be valiant men and valued women, then we need to take note of those who are leading the life they've been given and imitate them, so that one day *we* can be worthy of imitation. Do you see the importance of replication here? We imitate leaders so that we can become leaders who are worthy of imitation – for all those who will imitate us.

This idea of being worthy of imitation can be applied to every person, in every life situation. Let's consider a single woman. A single woman who wants to become a valued woman would be very wise to plug into the community of a Gospel-centered church. This is *not* because the church is some magical place where good people suddenly become better through a set of ritual practices. Rather, the church (or, at least, a good church) is a community of grace where broken people can walk in the light together and grow in love and obedience to God, and love for one another. If a single woman wants to find some women to imitate, she should start by looking here.

As she begins to form relationships with other women, built upon kindness, honesty, openness and *real* love, she will soon begin to see where she is in need of *discipline.* This will naturally happen because this is what God does in Gospel-centered communities.[2] His chosen vehicle for connecting people to Jesus and redeeming brokenness *is the church*, as odd as that may sound to you.[3] There are many churches where you won't find this kind of life, but that's only because there is no Gospel life to be found there. A church that is not built upon the full council of God's Word is like a low-grade cheese: It may be called cheese and even look like cheese, but the taste left in your mouth tells you otherwise.

    The whole point of this is to impress upon you the great importance of finding people worthy of imitation. The single woman must find valued women who are confident in their identity – graceful and gentle with others – the kind of women who draw the best out of the men around them. She needs to observe women who do not stake their worth on the vapid impressions of worldly men who don't know how to value women rightly. She needs to spend time with women who walk in the light and are ready and willing to expose their basement baggage for the growth and care of younger ladies.

    There is a purpose for this community, and it's rather simple to understand. One day this woman will become the one who is being imitated. Just as she received, she will give to those who need her guidance, and *age has nothing to do with it*. Depending on your context, you may be quite young, and yet still a model for other women – and why should we expect anything less?[4] Are you putting off your responsibility to lead because of your age? Everyone would be much better off if we'd stop prolonging aimless adolescence and start encouraging everyone to become worthy of imitation, wherever they are in life.

Are you Worthy of Imitation?

∞●∞●∞●∞●∞●∞●∞●∞

All this talk about plugging into a church may have caused you some discomfort. If it has, then I understand your distress. Perhaps you've always thought that churches are supposed to be full of good people, and yet you may know a lot of lackluster people who are always talking about their church. The idea that churches should be full of good people is a common expectation, but it's a rather short-sighted sentiment.

An aspect of Jesus' ministry that consistently repulsed the straight-laced, religious people was his uncanny ability to appeal to the common person. Ordinary, ruddy tradesmen were drawn to Jesus. Single women with very little social status were drawn to Jesus. Tax collectors, prostitutes and others who were treated like outsiders were drawn to Jesus. Jesus was always engaging people who lived on the margins of society, people who were rough around the edges, people who the religious leaders usually tried to avoid.[5]

Eventually, the religious leaders came to the conclusion that Jesus was a sinner, a drunkard, and an all-around mischief-maker because he spent much of his time with people who lived in all kinds of habitual sin. What those Pharisees and Scribes didn't see, though, was how Jesus was making those sinners into new men and new women. When Jesus first welcomed them into his company, they were quite unfit for any kind of leadership. But somehow, over time, these people were changed.

Jesus' ministry was remarkable precisely because he appealed to 'bad' people.[6] Many assumed this was because he condoned bad behavior, but this was not the case, at all. On the contrary, they were drawn to Jesus because he lovingly warned them how *serious* their sin was – and at the same time – how they could be *free* from it if they would follow him.[7] Do you see what Jesus was doing? He was inviting people who were not worthy of imitation to follow him, and then He showed them how to become worthy of imitation. Through the Holy Spirit, this is *still* what Jesus is doing in Gospel-centered churches today.

Here is the point of all this: Before you discount a church because you think it is full of hypocrites, you need to evaluate the legitimacy of your conclusion. If your issue with the church is that it is made up of many flawed people with many problems who don't appear all that good – then you're just beating a very old drum, in fact, the same drum the Pharisees played. Although you may not consider yourself 'religious,' your disdain for that uneducated rabble called the church reveals you're a first-class Pharisee, through and through.

What you really need to watch out for are churches that have abandoned Jesus' model of ministry.[8] Avoid churches that don't worship Jesus as God.[9] Avoid churches that reject the Trinity. Avoid churches that don't endorse the full counsel of the Bible.[10]

Some churches, for example, wish to do nothing but talk about the seriousness of certain sins, without, of course, ever addressing the seriousness of the sins *they* engage in. Instead of inviting broken people to join them so they can know the power of Jesus' grace and healing, they pretend like they're not broken and push everyone away who threatens to tarnish their 'holy' image.

On the other end, you can also find churches that wish to do nothing but *avoid* talking about sin, altogether. They talk about self-esteem and self-actualization, which are milder ways of saying what they actually teach, which is

Are you Worthy of Imitation?

self-worship.[11] These churches certainly appeal to those who need the power of Jesus' grace and healing, but you won't find any of that power there. When Jesus invited people to join him, he wasn't just helping them find a place to belong; he was showing them how to become worthy of imitation. He was freeing them from their belonging to sinful passions, and showing them how to belong to a holy God.

So be wary of churches that have abandoned Jesus' model of ministry; at the same time, be wary of your personal pride, which has driven many people away from healthy churches.

∞●∞●∞●∞●∞●∞●∞●∞

If you're looking for a reason *why* you should become worthy of imitation, then look no further than Jesus' beautiful summarization of the law: *Love God with all your heart, mind, soul and body, and love other people as yourself.*[12] To become worthy of imitation is to live for the glory of God and the good of others. We work toward that goal, not so people will look to us, but rather, so they would look *beyond* us to see the God who changed us. We become an example, not so someone's sight will terminate on us, but so they will see what God can make of broken people.

To help you understand this concept of loving God and others with your worthy example, let's talk about *dating*. Within the context of dating, I don't think this point can be overemphasized. Let me explain to you what I mean. Whether or not you realize it, you are constantly modeling what it looks like to be a man or a woman to those around you. If you're a woman, then you are displaying some version of womanhood to everyone who interacts with you.

Likewise, if you're a man, then you are displaying some version of manhood to everyone who interacts with you. Regardless of whether you are single or married, you are setting a standard for others.

So how do young women decide if a young man is dateable material? Well, it's quite simple. They refer to their mental database of all the men who have invested in them (or taken from them) and that becomes their standard. Why would any young woman take issue with giving herself to an irresponsible boy if she's been raised her whole life by an irresponsible father? Why would any woman ditch a cute guy who can't seem to find any direction in life (except, of course, the way into her pants) when all the men she knows are fickle, uncommitted and bent on pleasing themselves?

The point should be rather clear. When men lead lives that are worthy of imitation for the good of others, women see what a man is *supposed* to look like, and boys learn how to become men by imitating them. A man's worthy example can *protect* a woman from unworthy men. If she's surrounded by men who set a good example for her, then she's far less likely to waste her time with guys who aren't ready to be responsible.

In the same way, when women lead lives that are worthy of imitation for the good of others, men see the lasting beauty of a valued woman who is not swooned by the superficial antics of boyish men, and girls learn how to become women by imitating them. *We love others well when we become worthy of imitation.*

Some of this will happen *un*intentionally, which is to say that people are always watching us and learning even if we don't recognize it. It is good for us to be unintentional examples to others, but it is best when we *intentionally* engage people as Jesus did and encourage them to imitate us as we imitate Jesus. This is another reason why the church is so valuable. It's a community where you can commit yourself to learn from those who are qualified to lead, and set an example for those who are looking to you for guidance.

I hope you have already benefited from this book, but don't quit reading yet. We are just now getting to the main part. We've dealt with several issues, but we've yet to address the most significant issue at hand: What is the principal design behind this whole idea of valiant men and valued women? From where does it come? How significant is it? Now that we've waded through the less challenging end of the pool, it's time for us to jump into the deep end.

∞•∞•∞•∞•∞•∞•∞

Your Gender Matters, And so do You

∞•∞•∞•∞•∞•∞•∞

Valiant Men & Valued Women

You don't have to know much about history to know that gender equality has been an issue for a very long time. In fact, it's always been an issue. We tend to imagine that our contemporary times are vastly different from the past. In some ways they are, but not in the ways that really matter. Technology has changed, new theories exist and many societies have come and gone, but people have always been people. The desire in your heart to make your life all about you is the *same* desire that's plagued our race for a very long time. This selfish desire (which we could even call a curse) has played out in various ways throughout the ages. It has motivated wars and murder and adultery and greed, and it stands at the center of gender inequality.

Something about the Bible that astounds me is its insistence on gender equality, especially within historical cultures that traditionally subverted women. The Bible *insists* that men and women are equal in value, significance and purpose.

Now it could very well be that you don't agree with this assessment of the Bible; if this is so, then you might be operating under one of two *mis*understandings of the Bible. The first is that you could simply be misreading the Bible. The second is that you may have observed (and perhaps still observe) 'religious' men who make a practice of subverting women. Let's deal with these two reservations for a moment.

The Bible is, in many ways, a difficult book to read. This doesn't mean, however, that you need an education in Biblical studies to benefit from reading the Bible. God, in His grace, very often meets us where we are and applies the wisdom of His Word to our hearts. The Holy Spirit guides us into truth.[1] But there is some danger here; there are many parts of the Bible that are rather difficult to interpret.

Because the Bible claims to be the words of God, it's quite common for people to assume that a simple perusing of it should result in an immediate experience that confirms its authenticity. Reading the Bible generally does not work this way for a simple reason: the Bible is *both* the words of God *and* the words of people. Allow me to elaborate.

The Bible was written by various people at various times for various purposes, and each contribution (or book) was written to a certain audience. This means that reading the Bible well necessarily entails reading historical documents well, too. But the Bible claims to be more than just history. The Bible claims to be the very words of God – which is to say that God utilized human authors to write an accurate and timeless revelation of Himself for the good of all mankind.

In order to read the Bible well, you have to begin by reading it in its *historical context*. For example, you have to know how to read Hebraic historical narrative if you want to read the beginning of the Bible accurately. You cannot just read it however you like and expect to be doing it the right way. You must *learn* how to read it before you can read it well.

This is precisely why trained accountants are good at reading 1040s: They know how to read them correctly. You are free to interpret your tax forms however you like, but you can't use that as an excuse when the IRS comes knocking on your door. There is a *right* way to read your tax forms. In the same way, there is a right way to read Biblical literature.

Now, depending on your worldview, you may not believe we can trust the Bible as God's Word. But if this is true in your case, then you have even *less* of an excuse for failing to read the Bible well.

If you believe the Bible is nothing more than mere history, then at least have the intellectual decency to read it with the same care as you would any other extensive historical document *before* you argue against its authenticity. I don't quite understand how someone can be so sure that the Bible is merely a human product; yet *not* know how to read it correctly as a human product in the first place. You must learn how to read it accurately in its historical context and literary genre before you make your critique.

In like matter, it would be illogical to assume that a person who cannot tell time is capable of knowing whether a clock is set right. Learning the foundational skill of 'telling time' is necessary for evaluating the correctness of a clock. You must first learn how to read the clock, and then you

Valiant Men. Valued Women.

may evaluate its accuracy and value. This same principle applies to evaluating the Bible.

∞●∞●∞●∞●∞●∞●∞●∞

In the Old Testament (the first 39 books of the Bible) there are several references to men who engaged in polygamy. This is especially noticeable in *Genesis*, the first book of the Bible. Jacob, for example, married *sisters*. His first wife, Leah, was a woman he didn't even want to marry. His second wife, Rachel, was Leah's younger and more attractive sister. Scripture is rather clear that Leah did not enjoy her marriage to Jacob. Even though Jacob was a very poor husband to Leah, God still blessed Jacob with twelve sons who became the fathers of the twelve tribes of Israel.

When you read the story of Jacob, you can't help but notice that he was a first-class shyster. He deceived his blind father so he could steal his brother's birthright. He also deceived his father-in-law and swindled him out of a slew of livestock.

Jacob wasn't the only deceiver in his story, though. His father-in-law, Laban, was also a pretty slippery fellow. Laban was the father of Leah and Rachel, and Rachel was Jacob's dream girl. Jacob promised to work seven years for Laban in return for Rachel's hand in marriage. But when the seven years had come, Laban gave *Leah* to Jacob instead. Jacob protested, and Laban told him he could have Rachel too – in return, of course, for *another* seven years of labor. Jacob agreed. The Bible says that Jacob loved Rachel more than he loved Leah.[2]

Now how would you feel if you were Leah? Her father gave her to a man who didn't even want her in order to procure seven years of cheap labor, while her husband married her only because he *had to* in order to be with his dream girl, Leah's younger sister. Leah, a precious woman, was reduced to a cheap commodity. Two men used her to get what they really wanted. Would you call this gender inequality? I most certainly would.

This is where people often get confused because they are *mis*reading the Bible. They assume that the Bible endorses gender inequality because a 'father of the faith' like Jacob used and mistreated a woman. Jacob *did* use and mistreat Leah, but the Bible does *not* endorse that behavior. The Bible frowns upon it.

If you can't see this in the Bible, then it's because you haven't yet learned how to read Hebraic historical narrative. In the book of Genesis, the narrator doesn't step out of the story to make moral statements. Instead, the reader is supposed to *draw out* the moral implications by closely following the story. What you may notice about Jacob's story is that his marriage to two women caused all kinds of pain to everyone involved: Jacob, Leah, Rachel and all the children. Jacob's sin of idolizing Rachel and mistreating Leah and deceiving people eventually caught up to him.

Some have asked (and continue to ask), 'Then why did God make Jacob the father of the twelve tribes of Israel and bless him in so many ways?' It's a valid question, but you're only asking it because you're out of touch with your *own* sin. Why does God bless you or me with *anything*? Why does God give sinful people good things? Why does God work through broken people? Here's a hint: It's not because we've earned it.

He loves, blesses and guides sinful people because He is an exceedingly kind God, full of grace and mercy.[3] And as for Leah, God did not abandon her. She found some solace when she was blessed with a very special child in the midst of her suffering. You'll have to read the story if you'd like to know more.[4]

The point of all this is to help you recognize that you could be misreading the Bible. If you think the Bible promotes gender *in*equality, then you're simply misreading it.

The second reservation we previously stated is somewhat tied to the first, and it is the argument that the Bible promotes gender inequality because many 'religious' men make a practice of subverting women. I do not doubt that this is absolutely true. But I also do not think it is a very strong argument. We, as a human race, are quite talented at corrupting good things. We use and abuse what is good in very bad ways to fulfill our selfish desires. In short, we sin.

What exacerbates *this* problem, however, is that 'religious' men mistreat women under the guise of a 'good work.' A pimp may beat a woman, but nobody expects anything more from a pimp. But a 'religious' man who mistreats a woman is held to a higher expectation – and rightly so.

Scripture is not silent about such people. Those who have justified their evil works under the banner of good works will not go unpunished. God will see to their destruction and damnation, and this applies to *both* the religious and the irreligious. Regardless of who you are, if you are disguising your dirty deeds done in the dark by parading around like a saint, then don't presume on God's kindness. His kindness is meant to lead you to repentance and change – not as an excuse for you to continue living selfishly.[5]

Toward the very beginning of the Bible, we meet the first two humans: Adam and Eve. God created both Adam and Eve, but He created Eve *after* Adam, and He created her *from* Adam.[6] This little bit of information has been misused by some men (the rotten ones) to assert that men are superior to women. This makes little sense, however, for a very simple reason. The first woman may have come from the first man, but ever since then, *every man has come from a woman*.

This is another illustration of why men and women are equal in their value, significance and purpose. Man was initially created before woman, but since Adam, no man has come into existence without a woman. Thus, men are not superior to women, and women are not superior to men.[7]

There is, however, something to be said about the creational order of the genders. God made Adam first, and then formed Eve from Adam. Why did God create Adam first? Why did God use some of Adam to make Eve, rather than making Eve just as He made Adam? The Bible says God made Adam from dust. It seems to reason that He could have made Eve the same way – but He didn't. He made Eve from Adam's rib.

This fascinating detail, found near the very beginning of the Bible, tells us something profound about the two genders. If we want to make some sense of it, then we need to consider how God viewed Adam's relationship to Eve.

∞●∞●∞●∞●∞●∞●∞

After God created Adam and Eve, he put on a wedding ceremony. He put them together as the first married couple. God created the first two people with their complementary genders, and then He fit them together –

literally and figuratively.[8] I'm sure the Garden of Eden was a nice wedding venue and a great honeymoon location!

It would be nice to think that Adam and Eve's marriage remained strong, but that's not what happened. A serpent got between them, quite literally. This serpent had a few provocative questions to ask, and ultimately, he sowed a distrust of God into the first two humans.[9] His target was Eve, and he succeeded in selling her a skewed worldview.

When Eve was deceived by the serpent, she began to believe that God was holding out on her. She started wondering why God told her and Adam to avoid that certain tree and its fruit. Was it really because God was looking out for them, or was it because God didn't want them to become all-knowing, as He was? The serpent convinced Eve that eating the fruit would make her 'like God,' thereby making God obsolete. She bought the lie and ate the fruit. Then Adam ate, as well.

But then, when God came walking into the garden to confront Adam and Eve after their sin, He did not address Eve first. Instead, He addressed Adam.[10] Now this seems rather odd, considering that Eve appears to be the one who was really at fault. *She* listened to the serpent, *she* ate the fruit, and then *she* handed it to her husband. It seems that Eve was the one who caused the disturbance. And yet, God called Adam to account first.

This detail provides for us a helpful insight into the purpose behind God's creational order of the two genders. As we've already stated, God created Adam first, and then created Eve from Adam. It would seem, therefore, that this purposeful ordering of the genders has something to do with *responsibility* and *accountability*. That is to say, when God made Eve from Adam, He was declaring a statement about Adam's responsibility *for* Eve and Adam's accountability *to* God for Eve's well-being.

Perhaps you are beginning to see what I'm trying to show you. If not, then maybe a few pointed questions will help. What was Adam doing when Eve was being deceived? Why was Adam not attacking the serpent? Where was Adam when all this went down? Why did Adam not say anything? *Why did Adam fail to protect his wife?*

What you may find rather amusing (in a sad way) is that Adam was right there while this took place. He just stood there. He watched his wife fall into ruin, instead of defending her from the enemy, and then passively followed her into the trap. Eve may have sinned first, but Adam was responsible for Eve and accountable to God for her well-being.

God required Adam to account for his sin first because Adam was supposed to protect and nourish his wife. This explains the significance of God's creational order of the genders. *This is why men must be valiant in order for women to be valued.* This is why man was made before woman. And this brief account of how sin entered the world helps us understand why so many women are repulsed at the idea of following a man. They have experienced the leadership (or lack thereof) of irresponsible, passive, self-serving, limp-wristed, insensitive men who cannot take care of themselves, much less lead and nurture a precious woman.

What I hope you are beginning to realize is that all the instances of gender inequality in the Bible are not there for the purpose of *promoting* it. In fact, the contrary is true. They are there for the purpose of explaining it, both its origins and terrible consequences. All the instances of gender inequality in the Bible stand in stark contrast to

Valiant Men. Valued Women.

God's creational order of the genders. *He* made it good. *We* made it bad.

∞●∞●∞●∞●∞●∞●∞●∞

I can imagine that some of you, especially some of you women, are not satisfied with this arrangement. Perhaps you find it rather silly that you *need* a man to be responsible for you. I couldn't agree more. I can tell you from experience that my wife doesn't need anyone to lead her – certainly not in any demeaning sense. She is perfectly capable of doing for herself all kinds of things, and more capable than me in many of them. If this describes how you feel, then I see your point – but you're missing *the* point.

My wife is a strong woman. She's a very capable woman, but my leadership for her has nothing to do with her capability. It has everything to do with her *value*. As a woman made in God's image, and the crowning achievement of His creation (for God, like all the best composers, saves the best for last), she is *worthy* of value.

She is worthy of protection. She is a wonderful creation who ought to be nurtured. She is a woman who deserves Godly leadership, not the kind of leadership that stands over someone, but a Christ-like leadership marked by humility and sacrifice. My wife should be valued because she is *valuable*. God saw fit to make me her husband, which means He has given me the responsibility of leading and nurturing her. She is a precious daughter of the King, and I am only filling in until her Father calls her home.

Now for all you single ladies, do not be dismayed. The fact that you are not married does *not* detract from your value. You are worthy of protection, too. You are a wonderful creation that ought to be nurtured, too. You are deserving of sacrificial, Christ-like leadership, too. But God, in this season of your life, and perhaps for all your life, means to accomplish this in other ways. This is, once again, why local churches are so significant in God's plan of providing for His people.

Valiant men should make for valued women, in every season of life – and this should be *especially* true in the church. Single women in the church should be honored. They should be served. Married men and single men alike should be cognizant of how the women in their midst are being treated. This is simply how a Gospel-centered community ought to function. God calls men to be valiant and to value women because women are inherently valuable.

In view of this discussion, I think a note of warning and encouragement is in order: If you're a single woman, and you desperately desire to be married, be careful lest you tie the knot with an unworthy suitor. *Don't make marriage your savior.* The attention of a boyish man may make you feel valued for a time, but you will soon realize (and realize too late) that he was valuing you as a self-serving adventurer values a foreign land. That is to say, his intention was not to help you flourish, but to rob you of your most precious treasures for his selfish gain.

If you fear you married a selfish man, then do not despair. *All married women are married to a selfish man.* All men are sinners like Adam; all women are sinners like Eve. Do not immediately assume you need to abandon your spouse. *Who* you need is Jesus, and *what* you need is the refining power of God's work in the community of a Gospel-centered church.

∞ • ∞ • ∞ • ∞ • ∞ • ∞ • ∞

I hope you are grasping why your gender matters, and why you matter very much, as well. Regardless of whether you're a man or a woman, your gender was given to you by a God who does everything with a purpose.[11]

We are now going to turn our attention specifically to *marriage*. Marriage is, by no means, a simple subject to study. It's rather hard to explain, and even harder to do. In fact, it's a lot like a dance, a very difficult dance. When you watch great dancers, you can't help but think what a privilege it would be to dance as well as they can. What is easily overlooked, however, is the simple reality that great dancers become great, not just because they desire the *privilege* of dancing well, but more importantly, because they embrace the *discipline* it requires.

Everyone knows that a dance is ruined if the dancers cannot finish well. It doesn't matter how smoothly it begins if it eventually falls apart. A great start is marred by a sorry finish. Marriage is no different; you must have the discipline to finish well.

The Dance of Marriage

Books on marriage are as common as books on dieting. You can find them everywhere. They plague bookstores like a cancer, wasting valuable shelf space that could house more helpful books. Cancer, after all, is a rather simple disease. It kills an otherwise healthy body by filling it with useless tissue. Self-help books are the useless tissue of the literary world, doing far more damage than good.

Shallow, faddish books about 'staying in love' and 'shedding pounds' crowd out better books, not because they help people, but because they *don't* help people. That's why publishers keep selling them. The only thing more profitable than selling a good product once is selling a bad one over and over. Most books on marriage are like a broken record: Always playing the same tune, and never playing it right.

The vast majority of books on marriage are virtually useless because they reduce the marital relationship to a set of trite, 'how-to' mechanics. They're all science and no art, and not even good science, at that. They treat marriage like a device.

But marriage is much more than a device. You cannot master it with a list of 'how-to' instructions. It's not a tool that exists for your self-fulfillment. Marriage is a dance; it's an extremely difficult dance. It's a living, moving, organic thing. It doesn't work just because a husband and a wife know what they *should* do. It only works when they are ready and willing to do it, regardless of the cost.

I know very little about dancing. I have virtually no technical knowledge about how any dance should be performed. But I do know this: good technique cannot compensate for a lack of discipline and passion. You can clearly tell when dancers are just going through the motions because all the life is drained out of their routine.

Many marriages have been reduced to this sad condition. There is no life in them. It's just two people living like strangers together: working jobs, feeding kids, finishing chores and hoping to avoid another fight. The passion is gone because the disciplines needed to arouse those passions are gone – or perhaps were never there.

A list of how-to mechanics cannot heal a marriage anymore than a list could teach someone how to dance. Marriage is just too nuanced and complicated; you cannot simply learn the steps or the music or the rhythm. All of these have to come together in profound way. Married people don't need a book of shallow, faddish advice. What they need is to understand the real beauty of marriage; they need to learn the dance.

∞•∞•∞•∞•∞•∞•∞•∞

Watching two people dance together is interesting because everything you observe in their dance is supposed to help you 'see' something deeper. A dance communicates unseen emotions like joy, sorrow, conviction and honesty. You cannot see these things in a dance, per se, but you can 'see' them *through* a dance. A dance communicates a deeper message.

You could even say that a dance is a symbol, which means a dance points to something beyond itself. This is, after all, the highest purpose of a dance. People don't pay good money at a theatre merely to see people dancing; they pay good money to see a good dance. Dance is an art form because it attempts to capture a concept or an ideal. It is a symbol of something greater.

For this very reason, marriage is a kind of dance. It is a symbol of something greater. The marriages that thrive are the ones that point beyond themselves. The most satisfying marriages are the ones that function to help others 'see' a deeper meaning. A marriage that does not point to something greater, but centers on itself never works because it's composed of self-centered people.

The fact of the matter is this: When you take something as monumental and mysterious as marriage and shrink it down to something that exists to fulfill *you*, you wring the life out of it. A marriage is not a device; it's a dance. Devices are things that we use to make our lives more convenient. Dancing is something we actively *do* with someone else; it requires our attention, discipline and passion. Dancing is anything but convenient.

Most marriages end in divorce because most marriages are about nothing more than just getting married and staying married. They're so drab. Marriage has lost its richer, deeper meaning in our culture. Marriage is supposed to be a symbol of something greater, which means it won't function correctly unless it's actually pointing beyond itself. Like all symbols, once people forget what they stand for, they lose their power to inspire.

In a moment we are going to discuss what marriage symbolizes. We will consider the highest purpose of marriage by considering what marriage is supposed to help us 'see.' But before we get there, I feel the need to say a few things about a four-letter word everyone says, but very few mean: *Love*. When we tell a person of romantic interest that we love them, what do we really mean to say? What do *you* mean to say when you speak this word?

∞ • ∞ • ∞ • ∞ • ∞ • ∞ • ∞ • ∞

Everyone wants to be wanted. You want to be wanted, and I want to be wanted. It is a perfectly normal desire. We want others to see who we are and to desire our presence. There is a reason why you have this desire, and there are healthy ways to channel it, but be careful. When this desire goes unchecked, it destroys the very heart of love.

The modern idea of love in our culture is quite pathetic. It's broken and twisted because it has been infected by a terrible case of self-centeredness. When people talk about 'finding love' these days, they aren't really talking about love, at all. Instead, they are talking about their desire to find someone who will want them. They constantly whine about it, going on and on about how much they want someone to love.

But they don't really desire love; they are using the word 'love,' but not using it correctly. What they desire is someone who will *want* them.

The heart of real love is costly sacrifice for the good of someone else. That's love at its finest.[1] Love does not motivate us to whine about how much we need someone to validate us. Love serves; it doesn't demand to be served.[2]

It is rather ironic when you think about it. You would suppose that those who constantly whine about 'finding someone to love' are infatuated with the idea of loving another person, but that's not the case. They are actually infatuated with *themselves*. They talk about how great they feel when someone 'loves' them, but they are woefully confused. Their need to be validated by someone else has consumed them. But love cannot truly exist in this environment because love is the opposite of self-centeredness.

I do not say these things to make you feel worse about yourself, but better. Why in the world are you looking for your identity in someone else? You won't find it in them, and you won't find it in you. *You're settling*. Your vision is far too narrow, and you are selling yourself short. You've made a god of yourself. You desperately want people to like you, to want you, to need you – to worship you, in a sense.

All of us need to understand that our desire to be wanted is not a sign of our strength, but of our *weakness*. We should use this desire as a reminder of our need for redemption. If we do, then it will serve us well. It will check our pride. We will come to realize, as we should, that we want someone to validate us because we have many insufficiencies. We need someone to love us because we are often *un*lovable.

This is a hard phenomenon to explain, but somehow, when we are emptied of ourselves, we start to think more about other people. This also works in the negative. When we focus too much on ourselves, we eventually become blind to everyone else.

I'm sure you can discern how this concept applies to marriage. If you view marriage as something that will serve *your* needs, then your marriage will fall apart. You will have this ridiculous expectation that your spouse must always make you feel a certain way; at the same time, you will become blind to how awful you make your spouse feel. You will become like a black hole – offering nothing and sucking the life out of everything.

Real love gives. Real love is costly. Real love inconveniences itself for the good of others. Love meets the needs of others before it pleases itself, and – more than this – real love finds its highest pleasure in serving others.[3] Love is a romantic thing. It should make us sing and dance and smile with a sparkle in our eye. But love is also as hard as nails. It's stronger than steel. It should weather the worst of storms. The softer aspects of love are built upon this hard foundation of self-sacrifice. You cannot enjoy the pleasures of love until you have embraced its inconveniences.

∞ • ∞ • ∞ • ∞ • ∞ • ∞ • ∞ • ∞

Marriage is, in fact, a colossal inconvenience. It's always getting in the way, but always in a good way. Perhaps you've never realized this before, but making a marital vow is essentially the act of promising to be *inconvenienced* for the good of your spouse. In a vow, you promise to be there in seasons of plenty and famine. You promise to make your spouse's well-being a priority over your own. You promise to keep your marriage even when you'd rather lose it. All of these promises could be boiled down to this: I promise to do all sorts of things that will greatly inconvenience me for the good of you.

I wonder if more people would wait to get married if vows were customarily given in such an unpolished manner. As a society, maybe we should dispense with the lofty language at the altar and use hard, simple words instead.

The truth is that a marriage simply cannot function unless it is about something far greater than personal fulfillment. Perhaps this sounds odd to you, but it really shouldn't. Getting married is the process of sacrificing what *you* want in order to give someone else what *they* want.

When young people who want to get married talk about getting married, they describe it as they would a convenience – they say it will make life simpler and easier and happier. They are in for a big surprise. It is akin to saying that you would like to run a race with your leg tethered to another person's in order to run *faster*. Tying two runners together will not make them run faster; on the contrary, they are likely to spend a lot of their time picking each other up after many painful falls. Likewise, adding the inconveniences of marriage to a couple will not make their life simpler and easier, but more complicated and difficult.

I am aware this doesn't paint a very colorful picture of marriage. I realize I'm making it sound rather bleak. But it's important that I empty your head of all the stupid stuff. There are so many stupid ideas about marriage, and the idea that marriage exists for your personal fulfillment is at the top of the list. Get that out of your thinking, or it will get you into a lot of heartache.

So why would anyone want to be inconvenienced in such an extreme way? What is the point of all this marriage business? There are many reasons to get married, many good reasons, but the reason that matters most is this one:

to point to something far more profound than marriage. Marriage is a symbol of something greater. If we don't understand what marriage symbolizes, then we won't understand the heart of marriage.

∞●∞●∞●∞●∞●∞●∞●∞

 Marriage is an incredible thing. It's a sweet joy. A healthy marriage is worth fighting for because a healthy marriage will enrich every part of your life. Marriage is an amazing privilege, but it is also a gigantic responsibility. These two parts come together. You don't get one without the other.
 Marriage is also a temporary thing. It is not forever. When a married person dies, his or her marriage ends.[4] As the old vow states, "'til death do us part." This is why marriage is a symbol. As you probably already know, symbols are temporary things that are only needed when the deeper reality they represent is too far-off to see. Symbols exist to capture an image of a deeper, unseen reality. They represent something more. Thus, a symbol is necessary only when what it symbolizes cannot be seen.
 When the deeper reality becomes apparent, the symbol becomes obsolete. When the real thing arrives, the temporary thing goes away. Marriage is a temporary symbol that will go away. It doesn't last forever because it symbolizes something that *does* last forever. So what does marriage symbolize?
 Marriage symbolizes the eternal union of Jesus Christ to the redeemed people of God.[5]
 Perhaps this is not what you had in mind. Maybe you were hoping to hear that marriage symbolizes some straightforward, idyllic concept like love or joy or

commitment. But that would be far too simple. Marriage is an extremely complex thing, and every symbol, by nature, is always *less* complex than the deeper reality it represents. As such, marriage cannot represent something simple and easy to understand. Marriage must represent something greater than itself, something not yet fully comprehensible.

When you think through the different pieces of the Gospel, you can't help but see the direct connections to marriage.

First, you have a God who chooses a people. He doesn't choose them because they are perfect, but instead because He finds them beautiful and desires to be their Provider and Protector. He chooses them simply because He desires to choose them.[6]

Second, this same God writes Himself into human history and sends an exact imprint of Himself, fully God and fully man, in the form of Jesus. Jesus is not an offshoot of God or a mere prophet – He *is* the eternal God of all creation.[7] Jesus came to love his people. He came to show us how far he is willing to go to make us beautiful, to wash away the stain of sin.

He lived a life free from sin and died an agonizing death to remove our sin. *Jesus paid our dowry with his blood*. Then he rose from the dead, never to die again, making our eternal salvation possible. Jesus satisfied God's wrath against our many sins by accepting the punishment for our sins, on our behalf.[8]

Third and finally, you have heaven, a reality that is – for those of you reading this – yet to fully arrive. Heaven is where God takes His people to be eternally united with Jesus. Heaven is an everlasting wedding feast. Heaven is where Jesus will continue to love us forever, serve us forever and fill us with unending joy.[9] We, in turn, will

Valiant Men. Valued Women.

worship Him perfectly, fulfilling the very purpose for which we were created. We will know Him fully, and we will love him to the uttermost. Jesus will forever be our Bridegroom. We will forever be his bride.

Do you feel as though I'm pushing the marriage allegory a little too far? If you do, it's only because you haven't read much of the Bible. The Bible regularly uses this kind of language to describe God's relationship to His people, and even in the New Testament Jesus is called our Bridegroom.[10] I'm not forcing this into the text; I'm only saying what it already says.

Can you now see how the Gospel directly connects to marriage? When a man chooses a woman to marry, he is choosing to be her provider and protector, to serve her with everything in him. A husband does not love his wife by pushing her around, but by dying – dying to himself and sacrificing what he wants in order to serve her.

He works to make her beautiful. He keeps his marital vow to her not because she's perfect, but because he chose her and he's a valiant man of his word. She responds to his love because his love enables her to function as intended. She senses her value in his presence because he values her well.

Through the mystery of marriage, they are made into one flesh. They become one. And the awesome beauty of sex points to the mystery of oneness with Christ. There is nothing more exhilarating than emotionally satisfying, spiritually rich and physically tantalizing sex within a healthy, God-honoring marriage. It's the one place where sex is always fresh because it's the one place where sex belongs. The highest purpose of sex is to direct our hearts to heaven – it is a foretaste of the exhilarating joys of heaven.

Husbands and wives are supposed to stay married until one of them dies because their marriage symbolizes the Gospel, which is all about a God and a people who will never be parted – not by sin or disaster or hardship. Marriage is built first on commitment and second on romance because God's promise to His people is an unbreakable covenant from which His passion flows. The vow upholds the romance; the romance never upholds the vow.

Don't you see? Marriage is a temporary dance that points to an eternal dance. Husbands and wives step into the dance of marriage to symbolize the everlasting dance of Jesus and his redeemed people. *Marriage is a dance that symbolizes a much greater one.*

∞ • ∞ • ∞ • ∞ • ∞ • ∞ • ∞ • ∞

I know that some of you reject the Christian worldview. To you, marriage has nothing to do with Jesus, and certainly nothing to do with the church. But I implore you to carefully consider what you've just read. Be aware of the reality that marriage only *thrives* when a man and a woman get married for a greater reason than simply getting married. If you want marriage to be all it could be, then you must accept that it is symbol of Christ and His church.

On the other hand, some of you have a Christian worldview, *except* when it comes to relationships and marriage. Perhaps you are listening to poorly written "Christian" music that is filling your mind with superficial ideas about marriage. Marriage is not mostly about you, or love, or finding the right one, or having someone to hold. It's mostly about Jesus and the church. It's about inconveniencing yourself to love your spouse, so that the world will see the Gospel in action.

 None of this is easy to do. It is very hard, just like a difficult dance. But it's the dance God has given us. We dance in marriage in order to point toward our eternal dance with Jesus. Marriage is, quite frankly, all about the Gospel. Marriage is an incredible gift, but it's still a symbol, and symbols only function properly when they point toward what they symbolize.

 Married people wear a wedding ring to symbolize their commitment to their spouse. It is a powerful symbol. It would be foolish to say a wedding ring means nothing because it's merely a symbol. It *is* a symbol, but it is a symbol of great importance because it symbolizes a very important commitment. We should treat marriage in a similar way. We honor marriage as a symbol not to devalue it, but to show how valuable it truly is.

∞•∞•∞•∞•∞•∞•∞•∞

 My wife, Ashley, and I have been married for eight years. We've been through seasons of ease and seasons of difficulty. Our marriage is rather young, but like all married people, we've weathered some intense storms together – many of them self-inflicted.

 As a married man who is writing a chapter on marriage, I think it's only appropriate for my wife to contribute to the work. So I have asked her to say whatever she would like, in regards to keeping a healthy marriage. What follows are her words.

∞•∞•∞•∞•∞•∞•∞•∞

When Ryan told me this chapter was titled *The Dance of Marriage,* images of Ryan and I slow dancing whirled through my mind. I recalled our first dance at our wedding – our semi-clumsy movements across the dance floor on a hot, July evening to a terrible rendition of Josh Groban's *You Raise Me Up.*

Although our dancing skills have not improved over the last eight years, God has grown and edified our marriage. It's a process that will continue until death does us part.

My mother and I have dedicated many hours to 'studying' the art of dance through a popular show in which professional dancers take on the task of whipping semi-famous people into 'real dancers.' I am sure Ryan would tell you that the few times he had to endure watching this show with me were excruciating. Nonetheless, because of my 'studies,' I feel informed enough to share my insights on dancing and how it relates to marriage.

If both partners in a dance try to lead, the results are confusing and messy, and there's a good chance they'll end up in a heap on the floor. Both are pushing and pulling in different directions, not working together but dancing separately like solo performers, linked only by matching outfits. Isn't this what happens in a marriage when both husband and wife struggle to take the helm?

Picture a couple on a dance floor and imagine the woman leading her man, sweeping him across the dance floor. Awkward? Yes. In marriage God intended for there to be one leader: The husband. When he leads as he should, his wife shines her *brightest.*

It is no secret that the role of submission in marriage is often viewed as demeaning. Some see submission as something a wife is coerced to do like when one fighter forces another to 'tap out' in the third round of a UFC match.

But when you see a good dance unfold before you, do you look at the man and think he is dominating because he is leading? Of course not. You view them as one, working together in beautiful, synchronized movements. Both have equally important and crucial roles. Marriage follows this same equation. When a husband and wife embrace their roles in marriage as God designed, they not only glorify God with their marriage, but they also serve each other well.

My mom and I must love dancing, or maybe we are just gluttons for punishment because one summer we signed up for a workout dance class. Our instructor taught us choreographed movements to hit pop-songs – and just when we felt like we had it all figured out – she would change the songs, and we'd feel like klutzy goofs all over again. Something similar happens in marriage.

You are going along, feeling like you're finally getting 'this marriage thing' all figured out, and then – BAM! – Emeril Lagasse shows up and throws spice into your noodle bowl.

Okay, so maybe not Emeril, but God does allow difficulties to arise in your marriage. He shows up and exposes sin in your life or your spouse's. He provides opportunities to learn and grow. Different seasons of life bring new dance steps to learn as a couple: children, new cities, new jobs, deaths, and so many more. You will never have the dance down perfectly, but Christ will help you learn better steps to take as a couple.

We must always remember that we are sinful people and that our spouse is a sinful person. We must have grace for our spouse as he or she stumble through the steps. Learning to forgive is an important part of marriage.

There are so many types of ballroom dances: Merengue, tango, quickstep, rumba, salsa – all uniquely different from one another. God gives us each different callings and different struggles. God made your marriage, and it is like no other marriage, so don't play the comparison game. Your dance through life is going to be uniquely yours as a married couple, but the goal of every marriage is the same: To bring glory to Christ Jesus and to portray the mystery of Christ and His church in the way you love, sacrifice, and serve one another every day. Enjoy learning and growing together through the grace of Jesus – and remember often those vows you swore to uphold on your wedding day.

You are not what you Feel

∞●∞●∞●∞●∞●∞●∞

     This particular chapter may not be well-received by many people. What I intend to say here will ruffle some feathers, but I am not doing it to be offensive. I want to be helpful. Nurses do not give injections to administer pain; they do it to administer medicine. The pain is just a necessary part of the process. Sometimes we must suffer discomfort to experience healing.
     This chapter may cause you some discomfort because we are going to discuss a very divisive issue: *Homosexuality*. Are you uncomfortable yet? I hope you are. Regardless of what you personally think about homosexuality and homoerotic behavior, you must readily admit that there are many people who vehemently disagree with your viewpoint. To experience discomfort during discussions such as this one is usually a good thing: It reveals you're not too ignorant to realize that what you say *does* affect other people.[1]

Generally speaking, I think it's not a good idea to pretend like you understand something you really don't understand. I understand what homosexuality is and what it is not, insofar as the definition of it goes. What I do not understand, however, is the experience of feeling sexual attraction to another man. For this reason, I will keep this chapter rather brief. I will not speak as though I am an expert on something that I am not.

I hope you didn't read that last statement as some sort of a moralistic power play. It was not. I do not think I am somehow superior to men who are sexually attracted to other men. I do not believe sexual attraction should define a person. I am a heterosexual, but more than that, I am a person. There is no such thing as homosexuals – only homosexual *persons*.

This needs to sink in before we jump into the meat of this discussion because we must *not* use this issue to create a false sense of distance between ourselves and others.[2] We shouldn't think of homosexuality as we would an alien life-form, acting as though homosexual persons are strange creatures. On the same token (and this isn't said enough), we also shouldn't demonize those who have serious reservations about homosexuality.

We are all *people*, created by a sovereign God and afflicted by the corruption of sin. The distance we try to create between ourselves and others with issues such as this one says nothing about our passion for 'social issues;' on the contrary, it only reveals how little we understand ourselves and how little we care for others.

You are not what you Feel

In recent history it has become rather noble for homosexual persons to publicly state their sexual orientation. It has become an act of heroism. As a culture, we applaud the bravery of a person who stands up against the oppressive beliefs of others.

There is, to be sure, much to be said about the bravery of homosexual persons who publicly proclaim their sexual orientation. It is very difficult to stand up against the beliefs of other people. It is not easy to make yourself a target, and going against the grain causes a lot of tension, conflict and hardship.

While I certainly know it requires great courage to stand up against the beliefs of others, I also know that courage doesn't create truth. Many have courageously stood up against the beliefs of others – and have been absolutely wrong; inspiring, but still wrong.

Just because someone is courageous enough to stand up against a great tide of oppression does not mean they are *right* in doing so. It's important that you acknowledge this truth because history shows we have a track record of following people who display inspiring courage. Sometimes their courage has been paired with truth, sometimes it has not. Either way, it's often their courage that attracts people, *not* the soundness of their message.

Martin Luther King, Jr. courageously inspired Americans to fight against the oppression of racism. Adolf Hitler courageously inspired Germans to fight against the oppression of the Versailles Treaty with all its economic, political and social sanctions. They were both courageous; they both gathered a large following; they both stood up against a tide of oppression; and they both left a significant legacy. The former left a legacy worth imitating; the latter, just the opposite.

I realize this is a rather extreme example, but I hope it illustrates my point: *Courage does not create truth.* You can be courageous about something that is entirely false and still inspire many people to follow you. You can create and sustain a movement with inspired courage. Whether or not that movement is *right* has very little to do with how many people get behind it.

∞●∞●∞●∞●∞●∞●∞●∞

By using the words "truth" and "right," I have brought a foreign element into this discussion. It's no longer customary to assume people think in such stark terms. Truth has become experiential and right is now relative, or at least that's how we're taught to think these days. We've moved beyond the oppression of black and white concepts such as truth and right – or have we?

From what I can tell, I'd say we haven't moved on at all. We've just changed the landscape. We talk about the fluid nature of truth when we're referring to groups of people, but when it comes to ourselves, there is only one truth. We've all created our own ideology, and it's as narrow-minded as any formal religion ever has been or ever will be.[3] We think that by rejecting the formal systems of truth (religions) we have thrown out the oppression of truth; not so. We've just created our own personal systems that are just as oppressive.

You cannot avoid oppression. It is everywhere. It guides our world. You're not floating in the air right now because of the oppression of gravity. It constantly holds you down, quite literally, and no matter how hard you shake your fist in contempt, gravity will not let you go.

You are not what you Feel

Laws are oppressive, even the minor ones. Speed limits tell you how fast you can drive. City ordinances tell you how late you can make noise. Tax tables tell you how much money you must send to the government. And environmental regulations tell you where you must dispose of your trash. All of us live in an ocean of oppression.

Most of the oppression we live under is not bad, but actually very *good*. Gravity protects our world from the chaos of everything and everyone floating everywhere. Speed limits protect children from getting run over by employees who are late for their shift. City noise ordinances protect citizens' ability to sleep. Tax tables protect our society from going into disrepair. And environmental regulations protect our planet from destructive pollution. These forms of oppression are good.

There are other types of oppression that are even more elemental and obvious than civil laws – one of them is your *gender*. Men and women naturally come with certain standard parts, which make us quite complementary. It takes very little imagination to put together how men and women fit together. And not only do our complementary parts fit, but they produce new life when united. Our gender is most certainly a form of oppression, which is to say it is something that *binds* us.

Now all this may sound a little silly; is it really necessary to conduct a sex education seminar right now? But if you think this is silly, it's only because you're too silly to see that it's not silly at all. Sometimes the truths closest to us are the easiest ones to overlook.[4] Our gender is a form of oppression, and it's a *good* thing. It's like gravity; it's there for a reason. It is something that promotes human flourishing. It protects our race from extinction. It is the basis of the family unit. I could go on.

Valiant Men. Valued Women.

When a homosexual person stands up against the oppression of traditional marriage and traditional sexual values, he or she is courageously standing up against a form of oppression – but that's not the real issue. Our culture talks as though it is the real issue, but it's not. The real issue is whether or not that oppression is a *bad* thing. The real issue is whether or not that oppression should be removed, or kept just as it is.

∞ • ∞ • ∞ • ∞ • ∞ • ∞ • ∞ • ∞

We live in an age of a very odd paradox. Everywhere around us science and technology are advancing everything. We are learning more and more about how the world works. We know Earth is the perfect distance from the sun so as to promote organic life, so we utilize incredible telescopes to look into space, wondering if we can find another planet that is the same distance from a far-off star.

We know how the human heart works, so when someone has a clogged artery we can cut into them and replace it with a perfect synthetic substitute. We even know how foods are flavored, so much so that we can make chemical flavorings, which cause little sugary beans to taste like whatever we like.

All this progress has been made by research, and all this research has been accomplished through reason. We learn how something works and then put together how to use it most effectively for human flourishing.

Homosexuality is a paradox in the midst of all this progress. It makes very little intellectual sense. As of late, there has been much discussion about homosexual persons raising children together. Many studies have been done to legitimize homosexual marriage by attempting to prove that

You are not what you Feel

children are not adversely affected by this arrangement. But are we not overlooking a rather obvious thing? Homosexual persons cannot produce a child. Should we be discussing whether or not it's good for children to have homosexual parents, or should we be discussing why we're overlooking the self-evident reality that homosexual persons cannot produce a child together in the first place?

Not to be too juvenile – but you could just as easily do a study on the effects of eating cereal with a fork. You would conclude that people can eat cereal with a fork and still ingest some milk. But this misses the point, entirely. Spoons were clearly designed to help us eat foods such as cereal. It is completely out of order to ask whether or not we can eat cereal with a fork before we ask why we are overlooking the obvious reality that spoons were *designed* for eating cereal.

Homosexual persons are applauded for standing up against traditional sexual values, but what are they really standing up against? They are standing up against a truth as old as time, a truth that cannot be avoided: Men and women were designed to be complementary.

After finally perfecting the light bulb, Thomas Edison said something to the effect of 'I never failed. I just found 10,000 ways that don't work.' It seems Edison's words have eluded us in the realm of our gender design. There is a clear design as to how men and women connect to one another. It is a design that promotes human flourishing, and it creates a natural family unit. It is the one and only way that works.

∞ • ∞ • ∞ • ∞ • ∞ • ∞ • ∞

I think homosexuality can be best explained *not* by discussing what we think, but what we feel. The truth is what we think determines how we feel just as readily as what we feel determines how we think. Allow me to explain.

When I think about fond memories, I feel the joy of them. As my mind recalls the sights, sounds and smells of long-past pleasures, I can feel the freedom of a full summer's day with no school. I can feel the exhilaration of my first date with my wife. What I think determines how I am feeling. All of us know this, and everyone talks about it. We are instructed by all the pop psychologists to think positively so we can feel good about ourselves and maintain a positive self-esteem.

What is not talked about nearly as often (but should be) is the reality that *what we feel can also determine how we think*. A strong, overwhelming feeling very often leads people to think in ways that rationalize that feeling.[5] Marital affairs commonly begin with a feeling – a feeling that is eventually justified in a person's thinking and acted upon. We like to talk about how 'reasoned' we are as human beings, but I think we're giving ourselves far too much credit. When our feelings cause us to adjust our thinking in order to *justify* those feelings, we have left the realm of reason.

Homosexuality is not reasonable in the sense that it does not promote human flourishing, and it disregards the obvious design of men and women. Homosexuality is not a sound ideology – it is a feeling that needs an ideology in order to be justified.

This issue of rationalizing feelings does not just pertain to homosexuality. People who rave on and on about God *hating* homosexual persons are in the same predicament. Their feelings determine their thinking, as well. They hold up signs with awful things written upon them in order to distance themselves from 'godless sinners;'

in the process, they show there is actually *no* distance between them and anyone else. And that goes for you and for me, too.

You are not any better than any other person, no matter how gay they are, no matter how much they hate other people, no matter how much money they hoard, no matter their political affiliation – you simply aren't any better. You're nothing special. You're not impressive. You're just another sinner who justifies your personal sin by raving about someone else's.[6]

∞●∞●∞●∞●∞●∞●∞

If you are an admittedly homosexual person or a person who has yet to tell anyone about your homosexual feelings, then you need to know that Jesus Christ came for you, too. He came for you the same way he came for everyone else. You are not a lost cause. You are not a worthless soul. You are not sub-human. You are created in the image of God, and you are precious in His sight.

The overwhelming sexual feelings you have for people of the same sex is *not* your identity. You are not merely a homosexual. You are a person, and you are more than those feelings.

You need to know that *you are not what you feel*. You need to know that even though your homoerotic feelings are very much real, they are not right.[7] You need to know that Jesus' grace is enough for you, and that God loves you, even if you have to deal with homoerotic feelings until the day you die.[8]

When I see our culture applauding a homosexual person for his or her courageous stand against the oppression of traditional sexual values, I don't see a victory

– I see a defeat. I see someone who has surrendered to the idea that he is what he feels. Jesus Christ came to prove that we are far more than what we feel. He came for people sick with sin, people like me.[9] Not to browbeat us, but to *die* for us. And in his death and resurrection, there is real power. That power is called the Gospel, and it's the only hope any of us have, regardless of our sexual orientation.[10]

The Gospel and your Gender

If we could please God on our own by obeying commands and doing good things, then Jesus' death on the cross was *worthless*.[1] That's a pretty stark statement and an abrupt way to begin this chapter – but it's the hard-as-nails truth. The Gospel hinges on the reality that we are incapable of making things right with God on our own.[2] His standard is far too high for us to achieve, and we're far too self-absorbed to believe there's something wrong with us.

All throughout his ministry, Jesus consistently said he came for sinners. He often told parables that contrasted a 'good' person with a 'bad' person. At the end of these parables, the bad person would be accepted by God and the good person would be rejected.[3] Jesus' point was clear: *Nobody is free from sin*. People who live within the illusion that they are good people care little for Jesus because they don't want someone to save them; they want someone to pat them on the back and reward them.

Those who recognize their innate sinfulness, however, have come to the end of themselves, and they are hungry for the grace and mercy of Jesus. They sense a need for a Savior, not a cosmic therapist. They want to be rid of their grievous sin against a holy God, not just their feelings of guilt and shame.

The Gospel is good news. It's not merely a way of thinking or a vague concept. It's a reality. The Gospel is a historical story about a man who was also God, who wrote himself into human history so he could die for our rebellion against the King of creation and reconcile us to himself.[4] The Gospel is good news because it's *real*.

The Gospel is the lynchpin of the Christian faith. It holds the Bible together. The Old Testament foreshadows the coming of Jesus and His Gospel, the four gospel accounts tell the story of the Gospel, and the rest of the New Testament unpacks the Gospel. Without this centerpiece of the Christian faith – without this cornerstone – Christianity is just another religion that tells people to obey commands and to do good things in order to please God.

∞●∞●∞●∞●∞●∞●∞●∞

When the Gospel is rightly understood, fully believed and effectively applied, it produces many good things. It helps us to let go of our pride. It causes us to feel compassion for others. It creates within us a strong courage to live in a way that makes much of Jesus. It fills us with hope for our eternal future. The Gospel is a powerful engine that propels Christians into Christ-centered thought, prayer and action.

But when the Gospel is not rightly understood, or not fully believed, or not effectively applied – the results are not so good. When we don't understand the Gospel or don't believe it or don't know how to apply it, we tend to fall into one of two common traps: *Legalism* or *License*.

People who engage in legalism emphasize the importance of justice, but they have a weak understanding of grace.[5] They know the significance of discipline and self-control and hard work, and they are motivated to live an honorable life because they recognize God demands it. But what they fail to see is that even their *best* efforts to please God are empty and hollow.

When legalistic people think about Jesus' death on the cross, they immediately think of God's justice against sin. What they fail to recognize is God's *grace* to sacrifice His only Son so sinners could be saved. Legalism overlooks the power of God's grace, and thus, legalists overlook the reality that *they* are sinners desperately in need of God's grace every day, every hour. The Gospel reminds us that we cannot be saved by anything less than the finished work of Jesus on the cross. Legalism, however, teaches us to *save ourselves* with our good conduct.

As a result, legalism causes us to feel contempt for people who don't seem to care about their own conduct. Rather than seeking to serve those who have yet to understand, believe and apply the Gospel, legalists push outsiders away. They tell people to clean themselves up so God will love them, completely overlooking the fact that God did not wait for us to become good before he gave us Jesus – God gave us Jesus while we *hated* Him. God, in his amazing grace, came to seek us and save us when we wanted nothing to do with him. Legalists overlook this truth because they don't understand that God saves people according to His grace, not according to their works.[6]

Legalism often looks good on the outside, but it rots a person on the inside. Legalists block the way to God and turn people away from Jesus by demanding that sinners must clean themselves *before* they can go to Jesus. Legalism is a broken gospel, and it has no power to save anyone.

People who engage in *license*, on the other hand, emphasize the importance of grace, but they have a weak understanding of justice.[7] They know the importance of accepting others and not being judgmental and loving people without strict conditions, but what they fail to see is that God gives us grace *to make us right with Him*, not just to make us feel better about our shortcomings.

When licentious people think about Jesus' death on the cross, they immediately think of God's grace to forgive sin. What they fail to recognize is God's *justice*, which is why He sent Jesus to be crucified in the first place. Jesus died so the punishment for our sin would be enforced. In His grace, God sent Jesus to be crucified *for our sins* so we could be free from condemnation. God's grace, therefore, is supposed to inspire our joyful obedience to Him.[8]

License overlooks the reality that our sin is a terrible problem, so terrible that Jesus had to die in order to atone for it. License teaches us to downplay the seriousness of our sin by believing in a cheap forgiveness that doesn't make us better, but only makes us feel better about never becoming better.

As a result, license is powerless to produce God-glorifying action in us. Rather than being inspired by God's grace to obey God and to make much of Jesus, licentious people empty grace of its power and misuse it to placate their conscience. License empties the Gospel of its power by reducing the aim of the Gospel to mere acceptance, rather than acceptance that produces real, lasting change.

License offers a cheap grace that encourages people to stay in love with their sin without feeling shame. License, like Legalism, is a broken gospel, and it has no power to save anyone.

At the center of both Legalism and License is pride and self-worship. Both of these are destructive, self-centered mutations of the Gospel. One is not better than the other. The Gospel is most certainly the story of God's amazing grace, but God's grace is supposed to make us a people of justice who joyfully obey God.

We should recognize both God's justice *and* God's grace on the cross. Jesus died to free us from our sin, and He has freed us *so that* we would be a changed people who live noble lives in a world of corruption.

In short, God's justice should cause you to love His grace; and God's grace should make you a person of holiness and justice.

∞●∞●∞●∞●∞●∞●∞●∞

We cannot separate our need to know, believe and apply the Gospel from our desire to become valiant men and valued women. These two things are inextricably linked. If we threw out the Gospel and just talked about how to become good men and good women, we would fall prey to either legalism or license.

Some of us (the legalistic ones) would grit our teeth, harden our hearts and beat all kinds of discipline into ourselves, only to find we have pushed everyone away because we are graceless, angry, worn-out and short-tempered. In our self-centered strivings to be valiant men or valued women, we would teach other people exactly what they should *not* be. Instead of inviting others to learn from us and with us, we would only befriend people with the same legalistic tendencies. Our efforts would be meaningless. Jesus would not be glorified, people would not be loved well, and our hope would rest in our feeble ability to be good enough.

Others of us (the licentious ones) would find ways to redefine manhood and womanhood so everyone could be accepted as a valiant man or a valued woman. We would emphasize the importance of acceptance and love without conditions. And in the process, we would teach people how to settle for complacency, marking off their womanhood or manhood as a place where the Gospel is not allowed to enter, let alone change. We would talk about the power of God's grace, but our message would be powerless to change anyone – including ourselves.

The Gospel not only shows us how to be valiant men and valued women, but it also gives us the spiritual power to do so. The Gospel shows us the significance of our gender, and it also gives us the right motivation to live out our gender in a way that glorifies Jesus and loves others well.

You can reduce this quest to a merely humanitarian one, if you want; you can talk on and on about the importance of us being good men and good women without ever talking about Jesus or the Gospel – but it would all be powerless talk aimed at an unachievable end. The moralistic folks would choose one broken road, and the relativistic folks would choose the other. But *both* roads lead to futility and death. We need the Gospel to become men and women of real significance. We need to understand the Gospel, believe the Gospel and apply the Gospel.

∞•∞•∞•∞•∞•∞•∞

This discussion of valiant men and valued women is important because it emphasizes our need to move beyond an intellectual understanding of manhood and womanhood into a robust, daily practice. It's not enough to learn why you should live out your gender in a way that glorifies God and serves others well. You must actually *live* it. You must boldly step into the complexity of your daily life and live in a manner worthy of your calling.[9]

It will not be easy, nor will you ever 'arrive.' If you're looking for easy, then I recommend you stay away from any real relationships with anyone. You can build your life around no one but yourself, but don't be surprised when you realize it's devoid of meaning and not much worth living.

If you're a man, then God is calling you to be valiant. I don't care how old you are – God is calling *you*. God designed you to be responsible and reliable. God has equipped you to carry burdens for the good of others. It's your calling. If you desire to show a woman you value her, then become valiant. Don't just tell her she is precious in your sight – prove it by fully embracing your God-given calling as a man. Be valiant as you were designed to be, by realizing you were never intended to reach this end on your own – or for your own glory.

Find your joy in serving and loving others – and know that God loves you. Remember often how Jesus carried the burden of your sin, so you can be strengthened to joyfully carry burdens for others. For the sake of your family, your church, your community, and all the men and women who will learn from your example: *Be valiant.*

If you're a woman, then God *deeply* values you, and why should He not? He created Eve after Adam because He saved the best for last. You are valuable. God is calling you to be an image of His hidden beauty. Your beauty is not wrapped up in your physical appearance; your beauty is found in the depth of your spirit. Be *secure* in Christ. Embrace the love of Jesus to tame your wild heart and to fulfill its every desire. Recognize *your* value in Christ, and be a valued woman who draws more than looks – be a woman who draws the best out of the men around you.

When you walk through seasons of difficulty and feel like you're surrounded by men who are not valiant, remember that Jesus is *always* valiant for *you*. Your hope is in Christ. Gracefully call the men in your life out of their sin. Remind them of their God-given calling to be valiant. But don't build your foundation on the affections of mere men. You are too precious for that. Jesus is your God. He is your eternal Bridegroom. Let His love for you define you. You are valuable, so live like a valued woman.

∞●∞●∞●∞●∞●∞●∞●∞

This book has not been an exhaustive study on manhood and womanhood. It's really just a conversation starter. It's a small book of big truths that need to be understood, believed and applied in your life.

The rest of this book has been written to aid you in that endeavor. A small collection of men and women, just like you, have made a contribution to this book so you could learn from them and with them. I hope it blesses you in your ongoing journey to become a valiant man or a valued woman.

As Iron Sharpens Iron:

Contributions from Members of The Seed Church

Single, but Never Alone

A chapter by: Brooke Johnson

A Single Woman's Mind

All I have ever known is singleness. At twenty-seven, I can't speak for all single women, but I can speak to what I've gleaned over those years. So let's catch a glimpse of the single woman's mind. For many of you, this may be new, but some of you will soon be nodding like a bobble-head out of pure agreement.

For starters, we tend to be social creatures. We love going places together: restroom trips, showing up at someone's house, or walking into a wedding reception. Fear strikes us when we arrive solo. *Who will I sit by? Who will I talk to? Where do I go without looking like a loner? Everyone else knows each other; I'm the outsider!* We deeply need to belong. We like to know what to expect before arriving anywhere because going alone makes us more vulnerable. Social groups provide comfort and confidence.

Valiant Men. Valued Women.

Most girls also love to plan. We pre-plan our weddings in our young, pre-Pinterest days. Detailed changes happen with the tides of trends. It's a continual process of deciding on a gown, decor, the colors of bridesmaid's dresses, and who will wear them. We even pre-plan baby names before a man ever comes along. We like to control issues, ours and others.

We are emotional creatures, building attachments to fill our needy hearts. Salty tears are not equivalent to being emotional. Emotions leave us wanting to feel *anything*, good or bad. Those feelings move us to passion, causing invested action. This happens in every arena of life. For example, it's much easier for me to invest my time and attention into a sports team if I've created an emotional attachment to them. I learn where they're from, who they are, and their past and present struggles. Once that's established, I can cheer until my throat is hoarse.

It's the same in simple, daily decisions. What should I wear today? *I want to feel beautiful so I'll wear this outfit to catch passing glances from guys.* Which hall should I walk through at work today? *I want to boost my self-esteem so I'll pass by this guy's office because his flirtatious small talk makes me feel wanted.* Our emotional neediness intuitively drives us to emotionally charged behavior.

Single women live in the constant pull of wanting a relationship, yet wanting confidence in singleness. I dread the perpetual question, "So are you dating anyone?" It doesn't matter how it is worded, I cringe every time. I cringe because I don't want reminders of my singleness. Yet, I don't want a guy attached to my hip because I want to prove that I'm self-sufficient. At the core of womanhood we are needy, confused, controlling creatures. How do we move from flawed singleness to fulfilled singleness?

Looking up as I Grew up

God graciously built a firm foundation for my single heart by showing me valiant men. Meet three imperfect men, whose impact exploded in my life, setting the pace for my faith.

First, my Papa: When I visited my grandma and papa's house, I had several fascinations. The drawer reserved for grandkids and the oatmeal cream pies hidden in the cupboard were two of my favorites. The most fascinating thing, however, was my Papa's Bible open on the table next to his recliner.

Ingrained in my memory is my Papa unashamedly reading the Word. Papa constantly read and shared his opinions, whether people wanted to hear them or not. If he wasn't rattling off playful poems or calling grandkids humorous names while giving them a 'dustin' - the most loving spanking - then he was talking about Scripture or a recent sermon. My Papa said, "If a sermon doesn't end with the cross, then it's not a finished sermon!"

God gave me an example of how to devour the Bible. Papa could be stubbornly opinionated, sometimes offensive, but he left me fascinated with the Truth!

Next, my dad: From my first breath, I unknowingly rested in the arms of a man who would continually teach me how to serve. I have seen him serve my mom, family, friends, acquaintances, and strangers. If something needs to be done, he is usually doing it before anyone asks. As his daughter, I grew up watching him work hard to provide for our family, whether it was a long day at work or simply washing dishes after dinner. His hands and demeanor calmly serve.

This service could have spoiled me, but it didn't. Instead, my dad's leadership showed me how to serve and drew my heart to men who serve. I've witnessed both the good and the bad. I've seen men like my dad who sacrifice to put others first, and I've seen men who expect everything to be done for them. Hands down, I am more inspired by a man of service than a man who demands service. My dad's legacy is not one of perfection, but of perseverance.

Lastly, meet the youth pastor of my giggly, teen years: Brian. He started as the cool youth pastor whose stories attracted people like bugs to a light. People couldn't resist his personality, but that's not why I valued Brian. I valued Brian because he taught me how to lead when I thought I was incapable. He valued me and invested in me, even after walking through my bratty, needy, stuck-up, selfish, teen years.

I trusted him to teach me leadership because I observed how God changed him. Brian was one of the first men I remember publicizing his weaknesses in the rawest fashion. He continually publicized his flaws for people to relate to him, or to criticize him. He led by leaping, and others gradually dropped their superficial masks, exposing their own sins, as well. Brian taught me that I didn't have to be perfect, just willing. God takes everything I am NOT and fills it with everything He is.

All three of these men impacted me differently, but they exemplify the same thing: Valiance. They showed me security in Christ, they challenged me to live differently than the world, and they made me feel safe enough to make mistakes *and* to face them. None of these men would ever abandon me.

I have also been in the company of demanding, selfish, proud, arrogant, passive, indecisive boys disguised as men. These men leave me feeling exhausted and diminished. I love the valiant men in my life because they make me feel secure right where I am, yet they gracefully nudge me towards a changing heart that mirrors Christ.

So ladies, how do we move from flawed singleness to fulfilled singleness? As for my own journey, I had to begin by appreciating the valiant men God put in my life. When you recognize these men, let them teach you and lead you. You should be valued in your singleness because you are valuable!

A Good Standard Gone Wrong

Independent: the culturally-fitting definition in *The American Heritage College Dictionary* is "Not relying on others for support, care, or funds; self-supporting." Our culture praises independence. It can be good. Independent people often self-start, see problems, initiate solutions, and take on difficult tasks when no one else will. But our culture praises independence to an extreme, which can quickly become an unhealthy desire to not need anyone, ever! This mindset *will* scar you, especially if you're a single woman.

In middle school I observed awkward teens craving attention, guys and girls alike. Two people could date without ever talking or even actually going anywhere. Couples lasted two weeks, and then they each moved on to the next person.

I tended to stick with friends who were too awkward to approach a guy and be taken seriously – and this worked for me. But let's get real: We ALL had crushes; we played MASH to see who would end up in a Mansion, Apartment, Shack, or House with their dream guy.

Fast forward to high school: My independent mindset stuck with me as my friends began dating. I watched girls take different approaches with guys in this newfound world of relationship freedom.

Girl 'A' would date one guy after another. She loved having a guy wrapped around her waist all the time and would slip into a freaked-out depression when no one doted on her. Girl 'B' would date one guy long-term even if she *knew* he wasn't beneficial. She feared being alone. The comfort of the wrong thing outweighed the discomfort of the right thing. Girl 'C' desperately worked overtime to attract someone, even though she went unnoticed. She was shattered, but always hopeful that one day a guy would turn around and say, "Where have you been all my life?" While watching each type of girl play her game, I allowed Satan a foothold in my mind. I obsessed about my independence; it was my defense mechanism.

I started telling my family members, "I'm never getting married, and I'm never having kids! I don't need anyone to complete me!" I had watched too many 'good guys' and 'Christian guys' pressure my friends into places these girls swore they never wanted to be. It was confusing because these guys opposed the examples of the valiant men I grew up watching. I didn't want to be vulnerable or weak around un-valiant guys. It scared me, so I decided it would be better to take the pious, purity approach. I didn't need a guy to make me feel good about myself. My mantra was simple: "I'm waiting for God to bring along the right guy."

People praised me, but secretly Satan was twisting me into an independent, heartless wretch. I became judgmental – better and more together – than everybody else. There was no tolerance for girls who needed guys. I didn't understand their need to be needed. Ultimately, Satan scarred me in two major ways: He cultivated within me an obsessively independent nature, and he robbed me of the ability to love people. I refused to love someone, unless they were just like me. I still fight both scars today, even as God continues to heal me.

Be careful how you view singleness. Ask God to honestly reveal your mindset. Do you bitterly despise it and crave attention? Is it your idol? Are you reluctant to need someone? Ask Him to reshape your mindset, and He will expose you.

My New Identity: I am the Whore and the Prostitute

God began a slow and painful healing in my life totally unrelated to guy/girl relationships. The root problem was not how I viewed guys; the root problem was how I viewed God and myself. I viewed myself as perfect and in control, and God was just an emergency line, only to be used when I saw fit.

Several factors led to my healing, but two stick out the most. First, God shook my family when my mom was diagnosed with Progressive Multiple Sclerosis. As much as my dad served my family, my mom equally served us in demanding, tangible ways. When her nervous system started attacking itself, her physical service was immediately limited; my family felt the heavy burden.

As a control-freak-perfectionist I insisted on handling everything. Suddenly, I went from a naïve 17-year-old to an 18-year-old who ran a household and played 'soccer mom' and 'ballet mom,' all the while knowing I could never fill my mom's shoes. I realized I never had control of anything. I was overwhelmed.

Valiant Men. Valued Women.

Through my neediness God allowed me to see exactly who I was and more of who He is. God kept pointing my attention toward women in the Bible who were called prostitutes, whores, and 'women of the city.' I couldn't get away from Luke 7:36-50. Here was this woman with a sinful, public past showering an ugly cry all over Jesus' feet. In her desperation, she could only bring herself to wash the filthiest part of Jesus – his feet – with what she had: her tears, her hair, and her life savings of expensive ointment. She felt unworthy to do anything more.

My heart for this prostitute went deep. While reading her account, God magnified my sins even more. I was anything but perfect, and He was ultimate perfection! Many 'prestigious' men looked down on that woman, but Jesus did not. Jesus was the only valiant man – he looked directly into her eyes. He publicly admonished her, saying that her *many sins* were now forgiven, and as a result, she loved much. He spoke directly to her and said the sweetest, life-giving phrase: *Your sins are forgiven*. Those words became real to me. I could see my sins, which were many, because Jesus pointed them out – and he *forgave* me.

How did I begin to live in fulfilled singleness? Jesus exposed my need for him and shattered my independent nature. I was completed by one, perfect, valiant man: Jesus. No one else could satisfy me, not even myself. Suddenly, the way I related to God and people drastically changed.

A Guy is not the Starting Line of my Life

I titled this section with every ounce of humility God has given me. I didn't write it with bitterness or jealousy, but with love. Women, wrap your mind around this: A guy is not the starting line of your life! So many women think they need a guy to be fulfilled, as if he could redeem all their mundane activities and bring lasting satisfaction. Lies. False. Don't get me wrong, I have watched friends marry and start families, and I have learned to value the beauty of God in a marriage – but it's *not* when life begins.

Life begins when you start learning to love. A lawyer once asked Jesus how to inherit eternal life. Jesus threw the question back at him. The lawyer quoted the law and said that a person had to love God with all their heart, all their soul, all their strength, and all their mind, and love his neighbor as himself. Jesus told the lawyer he would truly live if he would do just that – love God and love people.

What does this look like in the real world? Here are some things I've found. In order to avoid pity parties when hanging out with my married, engaged or dating friends, I need a God-given pep talk to refocus my soul. Being reminded of His love and promises before venturing out with married women helps me to listen, learn from, and care about my friends rather than checking out when they talk about marriage or kids. I must intentionally choose to learn from people in different stages of life.

I need constant personal interaction with the Word and godly community. I'm a creature of habit and enjoy dissecting the Bible when I read it, but I don't always allow God to apply it to my life. His promises stick with me longer if Scripture rolls through my head during a run, or in silence on the way to work, or while reading it before I climb into bed, or when I pray for someone as I drift off to sleep.

My scars of independence make community hard for me. I never realized the importance of godly women calling my crap out until I experienced it. We learn to love when we see others' flaws, and instead of running away, we face them together, walking with mercy the way Christ walks with us.

Lastly, I am learning to put love into action by investing in whoever God gives me. I walked into my job as a high school English teacher five years ago and prayed for more than just a paycheck. The ministry God has given me is unimaginable! It exhausts me, but it's exhausting because God is continually teaching me how to love people. I am constantly reminded that even though my background is not like many of my students', we are all screwed up! The beauty is in recognizing our many sins and walking with each other in forgiveness.

When God overwhelms us with love for people, we find ourselves doing things that scare us. But we press on because God satisfies our lonely souls when we live to glorify Him and His Kingdom, here and now. I may be single, but He is before me, beside me, and behind me, valiantly protecting my steps.

Let Christ valiantly satisfy your single soul, rather than desperately trying to fill it with something temporary and flawed.

Choose the Harder Thing

A chapter by: Matt Hadsall

I find myself to be an expert in little to nothing, so writing this chapter on becoming a valiant man has proved to be a daunting task. Perhaps you didn't catch that, so I'll say it again: This chapter is all about how men become valiant, so pay attention men. Ladies, please do the same. While the message of this chapter may not be directly for you, it is still relevant. You are a daughter of the Most High God, and for your protection, you need to know what a valiant man looks like.

I hope this book, thus far, has helped you to understand that a man's valiance goes hand-in-hand with a woman's value. I pray that the words of this chapter would continue that effort by challenging and encouraging you, both men and women alike. I pray that God will use my story – my failures and my victories – to encourage you and to stretch you. Iron sharpening iron, right?

If we can agree that it's possible for men to become

valiant, then we must also agree that men are not naturally valiant. In using the word 'become,' we admit that men are not born valiant, but that they have to *become* valiant. For the purpose of this chapter, let's call the natural man a 'cowardly man.' Now this title may raise images of a lion skipping down a yellow brick road, but do not be fooled: Cowardly men are not that easy to spot. In fact, cowardly men can't even see their *own* cowardice, which causes them to wrongly assume they are valiant. All men tend to think they are valiant, but few really are.

I am learning more each day about what it means to be a valiant man, all by God's grace, and it has *not* been an easy process. It doesn't come naturally to me. Cowardice, on the other hand, has always come quite naturally to me, as it does to all men. As an extremely prideful man, it feels strange and even somewhat wrong to say that I am naturally a coward, but it's the truth – it's true for me and it's true for you.

All on my own, I have no valiance because valiance is not something that can be earned – it has to be received. I received my valiance from a man. This man is not only perfectly valiant, but He is also the *standard* by which we should judge all valiance. I have known Him for nearly my entire life, and at the age of ten, by the grace of God, I committed my life to living for His name. His name is Jesus, and He has given us the blueprint for *exactly* what it means to be a valiant man. Everything you will read in the following pages points to Him.

Journey with me now as we look deeper into this topic, and please read with care because this world is growing more and more desperate for men – men just like you – to put down the remote, to get off the couch, and to become valiant men.

The Problem

The problem that I face, and that all men face, is not that we desire to be cowards. You would be hard-pressed to find any young man who dreams about growing up and becoming a coward. All men *want* to be valiant. So then why are there so few valiant men in the world? An answer to this question can be found in the basic fundamentals of electricity, which I learned during my four-year electrical apprenticeship.

Current flow in an electrical system takes the path of least resistance. Electricity naturally looks for the easiest way out. Sound familiar? I am just like an electric current. The easier a task is, the more likely I am to do it – and vice versa. But this principle of electricity is not totally absolute. Say, for example, there are two different conductors of copper wire coming from the same source, and one is larger than the other. The larger wire would have less resistance than the smaller one, which means more of the current would flow through the larger wire – but not *all* of it. Some of it would take the smaller, harder path. A majority of the current would walk down the wide path, and a minority would choose the narrow one. Does that sound like a parable you've heard before?

In Matthew's gospel, Jesus told a parable about two paths: A wide and easy one, and a narrow and hard one. He said that most people choose the wide path, even though it leads to death, while very few choose the narrow one, which leads to life. Jesus spoke this parable to warn us of the danger of always choosing the easy thing. Choosing what's easy is natural to all of us, but it leads to destruction and death.

Here's the point: Even though all men desire to be

valiant, few of us become valiant because we naturally desire to walk the easiest path, just like electricity. To become valiant, we have to find the narrow path – the harder path – and we have to walk it. We can't just desire to become valiant, we have to commit ourselves and follow through.

There is a phrase I heard long ago that has always stuck with me: 'You are a product of your environment.' This statement is not absolutely true, but it is a general rule that speaks a measure of truth. When I think about that phrase, I think about some of my closest childhood friends.

Growing up I attended some of the most diverse schools in our city, and as a result, I became friends with a wide variety of people who came from a wide variety of backgrounds. Unfortunately, for the very best of my friends, this statement was (and in some cases, still is) their reality.

The need for valiant men is probably not felt anywhere more greatly than in the urban context. It is such a tragedy to see the vicious cycle of cowardly men breeding more cowardly men. With so few real men around to lead the next generation, young men are forced to look for manhood and masculinity in all the wrong places. These boys learn how to be men from athletes, musicians, and worst of all, their mothers. I'm not knocking on single mothers. I had one for years, until God blessed our family with a valiant man. I'm just pointing out that women were *never* meant to show boys how to become men on their own. It just isn't their job. Mothers play a huge role in the development of their boys, but this process should be headed up by a father. With no valiant men to show these boys what to do, they will become products of their environment, only to continue the cycle.

Today this problem has been magnified because

these boys are not only turned away from the narrow path of valiance, but they're also escorted to the wide path of cowardice. The world tells them that being a man means getting rich to serve yourself, sleeping with as many women as possible, and earning respect (by force if necessary), so they follow these patterns to feel like men – but they're not men. They're just overgrown boys. There is a shortage of valiant men, which means there is no one there to lovingly correct them. The cycle continues.

My Struggle for Valiance

I haven't just seen my friends become products of their environment. I've also experienced it firsthand. My biological father left when I was very young, so young that I have no memories of him and my mother together. Even though my older sister and I spent a few summers with him, I never really knew him. I could probably count on one hand the number of times I can remember seeing my biological father.

Not having a dad in my early years could have led me down a terrible path, but while my mother was single, I had a God-fearing grandfather who showed me by example what it meant to be valiant. Then my mother met the man who would eventually adopt me, and even though I was 18 when that happened, he has been my father and another example of valiance since I was eight. God blessed me by laying a foundation of valiant men early in my life, and I desperately needed it because a day would come when I would depart from it.

My fight began in my early twenties. I had more freedom and more opportunity to choose my own path. There was no more curfew from mom and dad, less of the "where are you?" phone calls, and much more opportunity for cowardice. I began running around with some childhood friends. It started off harmless enough: playing pool, trips to Kansas City for Chiefs' games – all the stuff that young, single guys do. But the more time I spent with these guys, the more I began to look and act like them. I was becoming a product of my environment. The two paths had been laid before me, and I had to choose. Despite the foundation of valiant men God had given me, I chose what was easy. I chose to be a coward.

What started out as harmless fun became destructive. I abandoned a Godly view of manhood and adopted a false, worldly one. I started going out two or three times a week for drinks with the guys. Eventually, a few drinks turned into drunken nights. Then, drunken nights turned into chasing women, and before I knew it, I was living in full-on cowardice. Every single time I chose to be a coward, I could feel the Holy Spirit directing me back to the narrow path, but I just couldn't listen. It was too difficult. The things of this world were so easy and enticing.

The road to valiance is not easy. Jesus was absolutely right when he said that the narrow way is hard. It leads to life, but it's *hard*. If anyone has ever told you that following Jesus is easy, then they told you a lie. Following Christ is the best decision you could ever make, but it is far from easy.

The Standard

If choosing valiance is such a difficult task, then how are we to do it? This is the question I tried to answer for myself over and over when I was living in cowardice. Every time I chose to be a coward, the examples of the valiant men in my life would come to the forefront of my mind, but it was never enough to make a difference. I felt guilt and shame for being a coward, but there seemed to be no power to help me change.

I would try so hard to be a valiant man, and it would work for a couple of weeks, maybe even a month, but then I was sprinting right back to the wide path. It wasn't until I started surrounding myself with God-fearing men that I began to realize I couldn't do it on my own. Becoming a valiant man begins right here, at the end of *yourself*. You have to recognize that you aren't enough, and never will be. You have to see your sin and your brokenness, and admit that you're a coward.

These words are harsh, but necessary. Many people today will tell you that you can do anything you put your mind to, if you will only try hard enough, but this simply isn't true. It doesn't work, especially when it comes to becoming a valiant man. But there is hope.

The answer is not what we need, but *who* we need, and who we need is a lowly carpenter from Galilee named Jesus. Jesus was already valiant before the foundation of the world was laid – He is eternally valiant. He came as a man and lived a life in direct opposition to the culture, especially the religious culture, and laid down His life so that we might gain it. Jesus is the standard of valiance because he perfectly did everything God commanded.

Jesus, the source of creation, became flesh and was hated by the very people He created. Most people thought Jesus was weak and feeble because he refused to make his life all about money or fame or worldly power. Jesus was valiant in the best way: He was valiant for people who didn't deserve his grace – people like you and me. He was executed because he was hated, and he was hated because he was the only real man in a world of cowards.

Valiant Men. Valued Women.

The work of Jesus Christ on the cross – His death and resurrection – is the ultimate act of valiance. This is the source of our salvation, and it is also the source of our *valiance*. In our weakness, He is our strength. We should look to Christ for examples of valiance in His life, and we should learn from Him. But we must do more than learn from Jesus; we have to trust Him. We have to give up on ourselves and give in to the grace of Jesus. Giving our battle to Him is an act of valiance in us.

Pursuing Righteousness

As we come to a close, let's think about how we can practically put our valiance into action. The first and most important thing you must do is learn to distinguish Godly manhood from worldly manhood. We must make great efforts to know God through His Word so we can differentiate true valiance from fake bravado. Remember, it is not always cut and dry. Jesus warns us to watch out for false teachers who appear to be good, but on the inside are like ravenous wolves. Cowardly men thrive on pretending like they are valiant, and they seek to lead others astray.

You need to devour God's Word. Growing in your valiance comes from knowing God better, and there is no better way to know God than through His Word. Men who don't know their Bible will not become valiant men. God's Word is *essential* to this process. Listening to your pastor on Sundays and your small group leader on Wednesdays is not enough. If your Bible is immaculate and looks like you just purchased it, you probably aren't in it enough.

Right now, in your mind, you may be making this classic excuse: 'I just don't have time to get in the Word every day.' If this describes you, then brace yourself for

Choose the Harder Thing

some loving rebuke: BALONEY! I know this excuse well because I've used it, too, but through the conviction of the Holy Spirit, I realized it was just that – an excuse. Your time in the word is *essential* to your valiance. It needs to become to you like eating food or drinking water, an absolute necessity. If you really believe you are too busy, then I want you to sit down and evaluate how you use your time. How much time do you waste watching mindless television? Playing video games? Working out? The list could go on and on. If we want to be able to distinguish true manhood from false manhood, we *must* know God's Word.

    I want to challenge you with something that has greatly affected my life and my pursuit of valiance. Remember when I told you that I tried to change myself by trying really hard, but never to any avail? It never worked because my efforts were all about me. They were self-centered.

    I finally found my success in the work of Christ, and by giving my cowardice to Him, I began to have victory over my sin. As I write this, I have not had a drop of alcohol in nearly four years. I also learned how to pursue a valued woman in a Godly manner. We've now been married for almost two years. The things that were my greatest failures, by God's grace, have become my greatest victories.

    This has not been a seamless transition for me. The transition from cowardice to valiance is not a one-step process; it's a lifetime commitment. Until this life is over, we will be faced daily with the opportunity to choose between valiance and cowardice. Don't lose heart when you choose cowardice, and trust me, you will still choose to be a coward from time to time. When you realize you've fallen back into your old ways, repent of it, but don't dwell on it.

    Too often, we dwell on our sins. Then patterns of sin

begin to reappear, and all we think about is not sinning, which actually makes it *worse*. When this happens, pursue righteousness. I've heard it said that for every time you think about your sin, you should think ten times about pursuing righteousness.

Remember that you don't have to be a product of your environment. You have the choice to fight for your valiance. You have the choice to become a man, but this only begins when you put your selfish desires to death. Jesus didn't promise ease. The journey will be tough, but the reward is unimaginable.

It cannot be overstated that this world is in desperate need of valiant men, and so now the choice is before you. Will you be valiant? Will you choose the harder thing? Our wives, children, siblings, parents and friends *need* men who are valiant. It is a sacrifice, a call to lay down the ease and comfort of what you want for the betterment of those around you. As Jesus said, there is no better way to love someone than to lay your life down for them.

Your Marriage Needs Community

A chapter by: Sean McCoskey

As Jesus breathed his final breath upon the cross, all of creation was shaken. A violent earthquake ripped through the ground, saints who had long been dead raised to life, and most importantly, the temple veil was torn. The curtain that separated the presence of God from His people was torn completely in half. For the first time, the Holy of Holies was not hidden. God Almighty, the very presence of YHWH, was now accessible to all people, for all time. Jesus died and brought the dead to life.

The resurrection of the dead at the time of Jesus' death fulfilled a purpose: It revealed what the power of Christ can do in the hearts of all God's chosen. This radical resurrection affirmed that Jesus was indeed the Son of God. How sweet is the thought that in that very moment, when heaven kissed earth through Jesus' death, the dead couldn't help but rise. Death had been defeated, and the grip of its power released. Death was obliterated by the life and love of Jesus.

This very moment you have complete access to God. This is only possible because of the divine condescension of Jesus Christ, who drank the cup of God's wrath for you, completely. The power of the Gospel today is no less invigorating and intoxicating than it was the very day the curtain was torn in two. Every facet of your life, every breath you take, and every second you live is impacted by the power of the Gospel.

So what does any of this have to do with marriage? That's a simple question to answer: It has *everything* to do with marriage.

A Gaping Hole

A few months ago I was halfway listening to a 'Christian' radio station when the topic of 'how to fix a broken marriage' came up. A woman was the first caller. Her marriage was on the ropes, and she was apparently the only one fighting for it. The radio talk-show host proceeded to encourage her, telling her that things would get better. He went on and on, reminding her that God is faithful, and that she only needed to keep her faith because God was going to make all things work out.

Of course, part of his reassurance was true, but I couldn't help but notice a gaping hole in his advice. I was getting fidgety, wishing I could have been the talk-show host for just a moment. I kept listening as his wisdom became more vacuous and unhelpful. He wasn't completely missing the Gospel because he did talk about Jesus' power to heal – but he never uttered a word about *community*. He never said a word about how badly her marriage needed the power of a Gospel-saturated community.

If you are married, then you may not want to hear what I'm about to say, but it's the hard truth: The moment you strip Gospel community away from your marriage is the moment you lose the greatest hope for healing and renewal within your marriage. Why? Because when you live in isolation, you remove one of the Holy Spirit's greatest means of communication. When you neglect your need for Gospel community, you destroy a great catalyst for change in your life. The *church*, or as I will call it in this chapter, a Gospel community, has an unmatched power to heal us and change us, but for a vast number of people its power and holy influence remains untapped.

Marriage and Community: Our Story

The easiest part of marriage is getting married. The hardest part of marriage is selecting a wall color for your house – just kidding. The hardest part is simply *being* married. Though I think most people wouldn't argue with this, our actions don't always indicate that we believe it. Our wedding culture says it all. We plan and plan to make sure our wedding day is perfect, and then we only set aside a day or two for premarital counseling. For every Benjamin we toss into our wedding-day bank account, we only invest a Lincoln in our actual marital relationship.

My sweet wife, Emilee, did the most wonderful job of coordinating our wedding. I did my best to help, but I think I did a better job of getting in the way. Wedding planning is not easy. It is expensive, time consuming, and laborious. For many women, planning a wedding comes naturally because they grew up dreaming about it and have looked forward to it for so long, but for most men, it's like trying to collect frogs in a bucket – not easy.

Anyone who's been married for a few years would tell you that the hard work of planning a wedding doesn't even compare to the hard work of keeping a healthy marriage. The wedding planning eventually ends, but working to build your marriage never ends. Throughout my few years of marital experience, I've counseled and guided some friends through their marital struggles. My counsel has never changed, and it never will—*seek Gospel community*.

Emilee and I belong to a Gospel Community at The Seed Church. Our leader's name is Pete, so we call it Pete's Gospel Community. It's a pretty simple thing. Every week we gather to pray, catch up and enjoy doing life with each other, and we alternate each week between what we call discussion nights and missional nights. On discussion nights we gather for the specific purpose of sharing how Sunday's sermon impacted us. On missional nights we do something that's conducive for inviting friends who perhaps don't know the grace of Jesus, like playing disc golf or grilling burgers and hanging out.

What I just described to you may sound trite, but it is far from that. Participating in the life of our church family has been the *single most powerful influence* on our marriage. It is where Emilee and I meet Jesus over and over again. We hear his voice through our friends who are grounded in the Word, and we experience His tenderness and provision as our Gospel community serves us and meets our felt needs, just as we seek to serve them. We have also received Godly discipline through the hard words we've received from our community. The quickest way to crumble our marriage would be to remove the church from it.

Go to Church

It's been said that 'it takes a village to raise a child.' Just so you know, Jesus taught about the significance of community long before anyone said that. In John 13:34-35 we find a new paradigm for community. The Apostle John wrote about a 'new commandment' Jesus had given: Love one another, as I have loved you. Jesus proclaimed that all people would know whether or not someone was really his disciple based on how well they loved others.

Jesus said this to prepare his disciples for when He would no longer be with them. Jesus would not always be with them in the flesh, so He taught them how to show His love to others. He taught them how to be the church! Jesus promised His disciples that when they gathered together in His name He would be there – working, saving, healing and restoring.

If you want to have a healthy marriage, then make the Creator of marriage the center of it – but realize that God will never be the center of your marriage until you become passionate about what He is passionate about: *The Church*. A Gospel community is the best place to grow in your relationship with Jesus *and* your spouse. You need a Gospel-centered church.

Where I Can't, My Church Can!

I can't even begin to tell of all the ways my church family has enriched me as a husband. I think of my big brother (the author of this book) who taught me that marriage would consistently teach me how selfish I am; he was right. I think of Matt who teaches me how to have a servant's heart for my wife. I am reminded of Rob and

Jordan from our Fort Worth, TX seminary days who taught Emilee and me more about marriage and church leadership than we could ever recount. Gospel community has been such a blessing to us.

On a fairly regular basis I am reminded that my wife has emotional and spiritual needs that I simply cannot fully meet. No one is capable of fully meeting all their spouse's needs. This is why her personal accountability time with other women is so important. Emilee's spiritual accountability and workout sessions with Rashell have enriched my sweet wife's heart in incredible ways.

In order to make much of His church, God gives us needs that can only be met through His church. I depend heavily on my Gospel community to enrich my wife and my marriage in ways I can't do alone. Where I can't, my church can!

As Emilee and I have grown in our faith in Jesus, our eyes have become more and more opened to the reality that participating in the church isn't merely about fulfilling a civic duty. Church is about so much more than just being a good citizen; it's about belonging to God by becoming a part of His people. We are called to live in compassionate community with our church because it is for the glory of God *and* our greatest good.

In John 17:3, Jesus essentially defined eternal life in this way: Eternal life is knowing the one, true God and His Son Jesus Christ. True life is *knowing God*, and knowing God happens through reading His Word and becoming a part of His people in the church.

Enriched in Everything, Lacking in Nothing

I am convinced that *every* marriage needs the power of a Gospel community. Marriages need community to endure hardships, to persevere through difficult loss, to stay firmly planted during times of plenty, and to remain focused on glorifying God and loving others.

In his first letter to the Corinthian church, the Apostle Paul wrote that he constantly thanked God for them. He thanked God for the grace of Jesus Christ, which had *enriched* the Corinthian Christians in *all* their speech and *all* their knowledge, and not only that, but they also lacked in nothing precisely because they sacrificially served each other. The church in Corinth was full of grace because they were deeply involved in their Gospel community. God was working in their midst because they were seeking to honor God by loving others in their church.

Perhaps you feel that your marriage (or any other relationship, for that matter) is currently less than stellar. Well, welcome to this fallen world. We're stricken with sin, and we live in a world where things just aren't the way they ought to be. But there is hope. Jesus loves you, and He is *for* you, as He demonstrated by His sacrificial death in *your* place. His death upon the cross can free you, and where that freedom can be best found, understood and applied is within His church, a Gospel community.

Emilee and I want to challenge you to fully experience being enriched in everything and lacking in nothing by knowing and loving God's church. We challenge you to invest in a Gospel community where you can grow in the Lord and understand more about what it looks like to be a valiant man or a valued woman. We challenge you to consider the following questions:

Are you participating in Gospel community? Who or what is having the greatest formative influence on your marriage right now? If you attend a church: Have your interactions with others caused you to know Jesus more fully, both in your personal life and your marriage? Be specific with names and praise God for those people!

Is God calling you to more fully commit to serving and loving His church for your good and His glory? What are you going to do about that?

Real Manhood and a Masquerade

∞•∞•∞•∞•∞•∞•∞•∞

A chapter by: Stephen Cyrus

"*Everyone wants to be Cary Grant. Even I want to be Cary Grant.*" -- Archibald Leach

 I'll never forget the first time I saw him. I was staying in Jamaica for the summer. My sister and I were supposed to be connecting with our roots; either that, or our parents just wanted to be rid of us for a while (now that I'm a parent, I definitely lean towards the latter). Either way, they had sent us away for the summer, hoping that an experience in our birth country would change us for the better.

 Well, when that summer was over I was changed, but not from the source they intended. I did get to know my relatives a little better, but that's not why I remember that summer in Jamaica. I remember it because of one, hot night in Kingston when I watched an old movie. The film was 'To Catch a Thief,' a Hitchcock classic, and in it I found my exemplar of manhood in a larger-than-life character. The character was John Robie, and he was embodied by the actor Cary Grant.

In the film, John Robie (Grant) is a highly successful and supposedly retired jewel thief who is being pursued by a beautiful heiress (Grace Kelly). Although Robie claims to be retired, she is convinced that he's behind a recent spate of high-profile burglaries. The movie plays out in the sun-soaked French Riviera, where Monsieur Robie traverses both the French underworld and high society without getting even a smudge on his perfectly tied neckerchief.

Cary Grant was a revelation. I had never seen his combination of wit, charm, and aplomb. Grant's John Robie was less about stealing things and more about being well-groomed, witty, unflappable and somewhat indifferent towards interested women. These ideals became my vision of manhood.

Masquerade

I loved Cary Grant, not just because of his style and panache, but also because of his ability to remain calm and cool in any situation. Grant's characters had an innate ability to handle any circumstance without getting into any real trouble. Of course, in a movie it always works this way because the plot is controlled by screenwriters who aren't going to let anything too bad happen to their main character.

At that time in my life, this was exactly how I felt about my relationship with God. I was His main character, and He wasn't going to let anything too bad happen to me; and even if something seemingly bad did happen, it would ultimately work out for good. I wasn't going to allow any kind of negativity (real or imagined) take away my calm, cool demeanor because, as far as I could tell, both God and Cary Grant would not have approved.

Having grown up in church with a childhood pretty much devoid of failure and loss, God's sovereign control of the universe was not something I struggled to accept. I completely believed that all things worked together for good, and I didn't let anything stress me out, ever. Needless to say, feeling negative emotions was rare and showing them even more so.

Believing in God's sovereignty is certainly a good thing, but at that time in my life, my 'belief' in God's sovereignty was really just passivity and indifference masquerading as belief. This proved to be a problem in the early stages of my marriage when I decided to leave my job and go back to school in pursuit of a dream.

Back to School

He ran as hard as he could. They would never catch him. He was like the wind. His teammates yelled excitedly as he streaked by. The boys on the opposing team couldn't even get within arm's reach. He didn't stop running until he reached the end zone. He spiked the ball and turned to bask in the adoration of his teammates. He had scored a touchdown!

Silence. A smattering of laughter. Only then did it dawn on him that those screams might not have been yells of encouragement. He was untouchable. He was uncatchable. He had scored a touchdown! Unfortunately, he scored it for the wrong team.

∞●∞●∞●∞●∞●∞●∞

I went back to school to pursue my passion – filmmaking – while my wife worked as a nurse. It was the perfect time to do it. She had just finished school, and I was more than ready to leave my current engineering career to pursue my dream. We had no other responsibilities, and there was a distinct possibility that we never would. We wanted kids, but we were having problems in the trying-to-have-kids department. It was within this framework of circumstances that we decided to make the bold switch.

We packed up, moved, and ultimately settled into a tiny, one-bedroom apartment. The first year went well, but something significant happened in my second year. I found myself gowned and gloved holding my first-born son. I realized that things would have to change, but I certainly didn't realize that my entire notion of manhood would need to change, too.

That tiny apartment got even smaller with a baby added to the mix (I'll never understand how something so small requires so much stuff). The transition to having a child and providing for the family was stressful for my wife. She made less money than I had in my previous job, and with the additional cost of the baby, money was tight. As any first-time parent knows, the stress level was high.

In the movies the leading man would have effortlessly charmed his wife. She would have come in upset from a long day, and he would have won her over with witty quips and trademark smiles. I tried those things because, to me, everything was fine. Bad things don't happen to the main characters. I would remind her that God was in control, and I would try to model that by showing no concern whatsoever about the lack of sleep and lack of money. After all, being a man, in my mind, was all about 'believing' in God's sovereignty and showing a good face no matter the circumstances. As you can imagine, my approach to her anxiety didn't work, and things continued to get worse between us.

While things were getting more difficult at home, I was really excelling at school. I graduated magna cum laude, and I was ready to change the world through cinematic storytelling. I felt like my time in school was a real success story. But looking back, I can see an eerie connection between my success in film school and my 'success' in my first flag-football game, in which I scored a touchdown for the wrong team. I had accomplished something great – or had I?

Great Start, Sorry Finish

He sat on the roof as the sun slowly dropped below the horizon, quietly viewing the city – his city. He still couldn't believe it. Instinctively, he reached up and touched his hair. He could still feel the warmth of the oil spreading over his scalp and the weight of that great man's hand on his shoulder. Even more so, he could feel the weight of the words that were spoken to him: 'The ALMIGHTY has chosen you.'

He looked over the city again, imagining all the good he would do for the people – for his people. He was a good master over his father's servants. Surely managing a nation couldn't be too much different. He had always been a leader. People had always followed him. Perhaps at first it was just his height that set him apart, but not anymore. He deserved to be a leader now.

He stretched his broad shoulders and wondered how long he had been sitting there. He needed to get some rest; tomorrow was going to be a big day. He was going to be king:

Valiant Men. Valued Women.

King Saul, to be exact. He smiled to himself; a man could get used to a title like that.

∞●∞●∞●∞●∞●∞●∞●∞

Let me step away from that tiny apartment for a minute. I want to flashback to my time as an engineer, back when my wife was still in nursing school, long before we were parents. You know, back when we held hands all the time and went to movies on weekdays.

I had been leading a college-age Sunday-school class and really enjoyed it. I especially enjoyed the opportunity to influence those students for the Kingdom. I taught the class by using a mix of storytelling and Bible reading. During that time I began to dream about what it would be like to expand that influence to other college-age kids, using that same formula of storytelling and Bible reading – but on a mass scale – and in my mind, the broadest, mass-market storytelling happened in film.

I prayed and fasted and became completely convinced that God was leading me to go back to school. I was so sure of the difference I would make for God's Kingdom. I was so excited because I felt like Paul at Mars Hill; I was going to meet people where they were by using film as a medium to speak truth in a relevant way. The future was so bright.

Bible stories can seem pretty tame when they're told with flannelgraph figures, but there's really nothing tame about Scripture, at all. The Bible is full of stories that are truly harrowing. During that season of my life, there were two Bible stories in particular that terrified me. The first was the story of Saul.

I'm talking about young Saul, not the Saul who threw spears at people during dinner and needed the harp to keep the demons at bay. I'm talking about the young Saul I described in the passage above; the young man who had a very bright future; the guy who was a head taller than everyone else; the freshly-anointed king of God's people; the well-groomed guy who not only looked the part, but was a good man, as well.

How did that broad-shouldered, handsome, Godly man descend into the madness that became King Saul's life? This story terrified me. The complete reversal of his life is so haunting. How does someone go from hero to zero so thoroughly? How could his life go in such an unpredictable direction? I read Saul's story and thought to myself: Could this happen to me?

The second story that alarmed me was King David's affair with Bathsheeba. David had been hand-selected by God to replace Saul because, according to God, David was a man after God's own heart. Think about that. Can you think of a better recommendation of someone's leadership or character? David was the real deal. So how did he find himself in that situation with Bathsheba?

David made many missteps along the way, but this was the one I fixated on: David was not where he was supposed to be. David found himself in sin, and he ultimately murdered an innocent man because he was out of his lane. He should have been off at war, leading his armies, but he was kicking it at the house. He was kicking it at the house and losing himself in the process. Instead of leading and protecting his soldiers, he was strong-arming a soldier's wife into his bed.

∞●∞●∞●∞●∞●∞●∞

Meanwhile, back at our tiny apartment things were getting worse. It had been three months since graduation, and I wasn't getting any closer to a job. A teacher told me the entertainment industry was a hard industry to break into and that people who were good would get a job in 6 months, or at least that was the average. That became the magic number in my head. It was only halftime; surely something would break loose in the next three months.

Add to that the rapidly-deteriorating relationship with my wife, and the pressure was ratcheted up tenfold. I had to find something soon. And as if the pressure wasn't already high enough, right about that time we discovered we were pregnant with our second child.

The questions began to spin in my head: Could I afford to wait much longer before finding something? At the same time, could I bail out on my dream when I was so close to seeing it through? Then again, was my dream even God-honoring, or had I become like David, selfishly kicking it at the house, out of my lane, and losing myself in the process? Was I really leading my wife and nourishing my family, or had I become like Saul who started out so well, but finished so poorly?

Be Caring and Be Active

Before I tell you how I answered those questions, let me back up and discuss a statement I made earlier when I was talking about my view of manhood. I stated that sometimes passivity and indifference can hide behind a 'belief' in God's sovereignty.

Let's pretend, for a moment, that you're a young, beautiful woman who ends up marrying someone who *seems* to have everything together. No matter the situation, your man is always confident and solid. You assume this is because he's organized and capable in any situation – but you later realize that he actually has no special ability to handle tough situations whatsoever. You eventually figure out that he's calm and collected only because he simply doesn't care about things very deeply and doesn't think his actions make much of a difference in the grand scheme of things.

What you took for confidence based on capability was actually indifference based on passivity. Talk about a bait and switch. If you're looking for desirable traits in a partner with whom you will face life's toughest problems, passivity and indifference are not good ones to look for. In fact, I would go so far as to say these are the type of traits you should *screen* for. Marriage is a crucible, where even solid people and solid relationships face tremendous pressure. When life gets really tough, a woman needs a guy who cares about the disaster of the day and acts accordingly.

I am in no way discounting the importance of placing your cares on God through prayer. Obviously, I believe that prayer is important and that God is able to answer prayer. But early in my marriage, my view of prayer was grounded in an unhealthy passivity that existed in my personality. Sheath a core of passivity within a veneer of Cary Grant's signature, unruffled appearance, and you get an empty shell of manhood without any power. It's like a vintage muscle car that looks the part but doesn't have an engine. It looks powerful, but you'd have to push it down the street to get groceries.

Jesus prayed and waited at times, but at other times he prayed and wept, he prayed and got angry, he prayed and

Valiant Men. Valued Women.

helped others. He wasn't passive or indifferent. He was engaged and caring.

∞ ● ∞ ● ∞ ● ∞ ● ∞ ● ∞ ● ∞ ● ∞

Cut back to our tiny apartment – a decision had to be made. Was I an artist or an engineer? I wish I could tell you that God clearly told me to stay the course and pursue my dream, or that He provided an equally dramatic admonition to stop shirking my responsibilities and just find a job, any job. But that's not what happened. I simply made a choice. There was no spotlight from heaven, no vision in the night. I prayed, and then I made a choice.

Looking back, I'm not sure if God cared whether I was an engineer or an artist. But I am sure of this: There were other things He cared about much more than my career. He cared about my understanding of manhood. He cared about how I valued my family, the precious people He had entrusted to me. He cared about opening my eyes to see that I was using the idea of His sovereignty to hide my passivity.

I learned there are enemies that cannot be defeated by any amount of wit, charm, or indifference. In fact, in talking to my wife about that time in our marriage, I realized that my carefully-cultivated indifference was probably the largest cause of strife between us. My calm and cool indifference was so intriguing to her when we dated, but within our marriage it was just infuriating.

During that season of our lives, she silently asked herself questions like: How can he be so calm when he doesn't have a job? Or when he can't provide for his family? Or when he listens to me complain about him, our situation

Real Manhood and a Masquerade

and our marriage? How can a marriage begin with so much promise and end up looking like this?

Here's the bottom line: Passivity and indifference may work for a scripted Cary Grant character (Cary Grant himself was married 5 times), but it won't work for *you* in a marriage or any other meaningful friendship. You have to care deeply, and not only that, you have to *show* that you care. Sometimes she just wanted to know that we were in it together, that we both felt concern, that she wasn't alone – that she was *valued*.

Be Valiant

At this point, I'd like to write a poetic story about manhood. I want to write about a well-groomed man who calmly addresses the disaster of the day, not with a quip and a smile, but with action. You know, something that involves him whipping off his immaculate neckerchief and laying it on the dirtiest substance imaginable, so his woman could walk across the filth unsullied. But that sounds like the third act in a romantic comedy, and that's just not how things really happen in our messy reality. So instead of making up a tidy story about manhood, I'll pick up with mine, starting from the day I found out we were having a second child.

That very day I called my old boss and asked him to be a reference because I was going to apply for an engineering job. But the reference wasn't necessary because he offered me a job on the spot, with an official offer following within a few weeks.

Was that the right thing to do? Was I now leading my armies again, protecting those who were entrusted to me? Was the ease of finding an engineering job after months of no job-leads a repudiation of what I thought I was called to do?

I don't know, but I do know this: Laying down my dream to love my family is what convinced my wife that I wasn't indifferent. She knew my passion for filmmaking, and she knew it was incredibly difficult for me to give it up, even temporarily, to head back to my old job, seemingly with my tail between my legs. Remarkably, I didn't feel that way. I wasn't ashamed. I sacrificed something very significant for my wife and my kids, and I *showed* them that I valued them above my dreams.

I felt valiant, and it had nothing to do with a ready quip or a trademark smile. I was valiant because I had valued others above myself. I was valiant because I was emotionally connected to those around me and actively pursuing their good and not my own. Manhood isn't about appearances; it's about the hard work between the lines. Manhood is all about passionately pursuing the good of others like Christ pursued ours, regardless of our personal dreams.

In retrospect, I can see that my lack of success in that season of life wasn't because I went back to school or because money was tight. Those circumstances only exacerbated the issues that were already there. The issue was my failure to value my wife and my lack of urgency in meeting her needs emotionally, as well as physically. This lesson in manhood was a painful one in many ways, but it was a gift from God.

There are trusts that need to be regained with my wife and dreams that I feel are still unfulfilled, but I haven't lost hope. God used these hardships to teach me true manhood, and this lesson couldn't have come any sooner, seeing that we've added another boy to the family. We now have two boys and one girl, all of whom need to know what it means to be a valiant man and what it looks like to value a woman. As their dad, it's my responsibility to model that for them. I pray they learn these lessons faster than I did.

Men, let me add a closing coda of encouragement. I hope it helps you on your journey towards true valiance.

Be Active. Be Caring. Be Valiant.

"*Everyone wants to be Cary Grant. Even I want to be Cary Grant.*" -- Archibald Leach (real name of the screen legend Cary Grant)

Multi-Generational Faithfulness

∞•∞•∞•∞•∞•∞•∞

A chapter by: Shanen Taylor

What do you know about your great-grandparents? Think about it. What do you really know? Perhaps you know their names (better than most) or maybe your parents still have a relic, heirloom, or some land from them. What was unique about them? What did they stand for, love, and care about? What were they willing to die for? Keep these questions in the back of your mind. We'll revisit them soon.

The idea of having a choice is very popular in our culture. It's American, individualistic, and laden with the connotations of our rights – our inalienable rights, no less. To *not* give someone the ability to choose would be, well, down-right un-American. Choice is a popular topic, perhaps even a mandatory topic these days.

Many years ago, sometime right around 1982, my parents made an important choice by not choosing anything at all. In case you were wondering: Yes, you can make a choice by not making one. When theologians describe the doctrine of sin, they talk about sins of commission and sins of omission. In the former, we choose something we should not; in the latter, we choose nothing at all. We idly sit back and fail to say or do something that should be said or done. Years ago, my parents made a choice by not making one.

My parents grew up in small towns in Texas and Illinois. They were raised in small, Baptist churches and attended a small Baptist college, now a university, in Ottawa, Kansas, just outside the Kansas City metropolitan area in the early 1960's. My parents were not allowed to miss any church events. My mother played the piano and organ, and she only missed a handful of Sundays over a twelve-year span. In college it was mandatory for them to complete rigorous ethical, moral, and theological training, including surveys on the Old and New Testaments. My parents were deeply entrenched in 'church' culture, but somehow their training did not help them think clearly about multi-generational faithfulness to the Lord. Allow me to explain.

Many years ago when I was a young child my parents chose to *not* make an important choice, and they instead deferred to my brother and me on the issue. We were heavily involved in sports, especially competitive soccer, and the demands of practice, games, and tournaments dominated our weekends. Something had to give. Sundays were getting really busy because they were tournament travel days. My parents decided to ask us if we wanted to attend church or just play sports. Like a softball question planted by a party-loyalist reporter at a White House press conference, we answered the question with ease. We chose sports.

This occurred sometime between my tenure in kindergarten and first grade, and it set my life on a certain path – a path my parents did not intend for me. My parents most certainly loved me and wanted the best for me, but I don't think they understood what they were doing when they asked us that question.

Now before you feel the need to write up any comments, blog posts, or e-mails, let me clearly explain what I am *not* saying. I don't blame my parents for every unwise decision I ever made. I don't blame them for the path I chose into adulthood. Additionally, I am *not* saying that organized sporting activities are evil. My parents influenced me, as all parents do, but I made my own poor decisions.

God placed several opportunities in my early life to know Him in a saving way. He beckoned me to quit worshiping myself and to start worshiping Him. As I accelerated into hedonism and self-actualization, God put many speed bumps in my path. There was the friend who invited me to church; the church lock-ins; the pretty girls who made me wonder if I should at least fake the church thing. I was so stubborn. My heart and mind were too hard and too closed to receive any of it. As the old adage goes, "those convinced against their will are of the same opinion still." All the way up into my early twenties I couldn't fathom being wrong (about anything), but I knew something was not right.

My worship of sports and my constant efforts to find my identity in the performance of those sports followed me throughout college and into adulthood. But as I approached the end of my collegiate career, the parties, the drunkenness, and the girls felt really empty. When I look back, I can clearly see I was desperately searching for significance. Painters have different sections of time or 'periods' to describe the development of their work. To

Valiant Men. Valued Women.

quote the band *Creed*, that was my, "what's this life for" period.
    Before I knew it, I was twenty-seven, married, equipped with a college degree, and working a good job. I was supposed to have this whole thing figured out. The scary thing is, from the outside looking in, it appeared that way. That's the dangerous thing about appearances; they are often only shadows of what is really happening.
    By God's grace, I eventually came to realize I was building my life on an empty, societal norm; namely, getting to that idyllic place in life where a person 'makes it.' For all my life, I had lived for temporary rewards.
    When we live for temporary rewards and put our hope in 'making it,' we invest ourselves in a losing proposition. Remember my questions about your great-grandparents? I'm willing to bet that little, if anything, remains of their accomplishments, no matter how celebrated they were in their day. I'm sure that little, if anything, remains of their possessions that are now decayed by weather, time, thieves, and apathy. All that really remains are the people they brought into this world by God's blessing and will. Their most powerful legacy is the people they left behind. This recognition is both empowering and humbling.
    It is empowering because all of us serve a greater purpose than we could possibly imagine. We live within an eternal chain of events foreordained by God, and we have the privilege of contributing to His eternal plan. But it's also humbling because it reminds us that God's number one priority is not you or me. He isn't overly concerned with the size of our house, or our waist, or when we'll get that promotion, or if we can afford some new gadget.

In order to curb our self-centeredness, we should remember often that God created us to serve as faithful links in His eternal chain of events. We are not merely recipients of God's grace; we are also *channels* of His grace who are supposed to prepare the way for all those who will follow us. This may seem anticlimactic, but consider the narrative of the Old Testament and how all of it builds up to the birth of Jesus Christ. God's redemptive plan for humanity centers on the *legacy of Jesus Christ* – His life, death and resurrection. The prophets of old were faithful because they prepared the way for those who would follow them; they didn't live for temporary rewards that would decay and disappear.

The Bible is, in many ways, a study in leaving a worthwhile legacy. It does not function to merely transmit information; it forms character and values and purpose in each generation for the glory of God and the good of others.

Perhaps your great-grandparents left such a legacy – a legacy that has stood the test of time. Unfortunately, this is not the norm. Most Americans, even Bible-believing, blood-bought Christians are not living with their legacy in mind. Many of us have been raised (and are now raising our own children) in a distracted, unintentional, meandering fashion. Here in America we can call ourselves Christians and function like atheists.

When God woke me up to my own selfish living, I didn't have a clue where to start, or where to go, or how to begin living a God-honoring life. By His grace, and His grace alone, He led my wife and me into the wisdom of His Word. We do not believe we are better than anyone else; on the contrary, God has clearly shown us that we aren't worthy of His love at all. But He chose us and saved us by His grace, not our efforts.

We have come to understand how crucially important it is to leave a good legacy. We don't want our children to wander as much as we did. We want to prepare them to raise children of their own, Lord willing, so they can faithfully contribute to God's eternal plan.

God has been so gracious to me throughout my life. All the small, broken, seemingly insignificant pieces of my past experiences have created the mosaic that is my life today. By God's grace, He called me to Himself in the midst of my rebellion. He softened my heart and opened my mind to hear and believe the Truth. I now see myself as a link in His eternal chain of events. God did not create me so I could live for myself. He created me to live for His glory and the good of others.

I know my wife and I will leave a legacy. We currently have four children, and God may bless us with more by means of birth or adoption. We will one day leave them behind. They are our legacy.

As James 4:14 states, our life is a mist. We are here one moment and gone the next. In the grand narrative of God's eternal plan, we take up so little space.

The truth is if you settle for temporary rewards, then your legacy will decay and disappear – and not making a choice as to what your life will be about *is* making a choice. You have chosen to do nothing. It's a sin of omission.

I think all of us would be wise to occasionally ask ourselves the following questions: What will my great-grandchildren say about me? What kind of a legacy will I leave behind?

Scripture Index

Pride No More
[1] James 1:14-15
[2] 2 Corinthians 11:14
[3] Romans 3:10-12
[4] Ezekiel 28:13-17
[5] James 4:6
[6] Ibid
[7] Matthew 16:25
[8] Ezekiel 36:25-27

Truth in Fairytales
[1] Mark 8:34
[2] Colossians 2:20-23
[3] Acts 20:28-30
[4] Romans 3:23
[5] Romans 5:8

The Heart of the Matter
[1] Genesis 2:15
[2] 1 Timothy 5:8
[3] 1 Peter 3:3-4
[4] Philippians 2:14-15

Walking in the Light
[1] Romans 12:1-2
[2] Deuteronomy 6:5
[3] Romans 8:1-4
[4] James 5:16
[5] Ephesians 5:8-14
[6] Mark 1:15
[7] Romans 10:13

Lead the Life you've been Given
[1] Hebrews 4:12-13
[2] 1 Corinthians 7:17
[3] 1 Corinthians 7:18-24
[4] Philippians 4:4-7
[5] Isaiah 55:9
[6] 1 Corinthians 7:23
[7] Galatians 4:8-9
[8] 1 Timothy 6:6

Valiant Men. Valued Women.

Are you Worthy of Imitation?
[1] Hebrews 13:7
[2] Hebrews 12:5-11
[3] 1 Corinthians 12:26-28
[4] 1 Timothy 4:12
[5] Luke 19:7-10
[6] 1 Timothy 1:15
[7] John 8:31-36
[8] 2 Peter 2:1-3
[9] 1 John 4:1-3
[10] 2 Timothy 3:16
[11] 2 Timothy 4:3
[12] Luke 10:25-28

Valiant Men & Valued Women
[1] John 16:12-14
[2] Genesis 29:21-30
[3] Ephesians 2:1-10
[4] Genesis 29:35
[5] Romans 2:1-5
[6] Genesis 2:21-22
[7] 1 Corinthians 11:11-12
[8] Genesis 2:24
[9] Genesis 3:1-7
[10] Genesis 3:9
[11] Proverbs 19:21

The Dance of Marriage
[1] John 15:12-13
[2] Mark 10:43-45
[3] 1 Corinthians 13:4-7
[4] Mark 12:25
[5] Ephesians 5:25-33
[6] Deuteronomy 7:6-8
[7] Hebrews 1:1-4
[8] 1 Peter 3:18
[9] Revelation 21:1-4
[10] John 3:28-30

You are not what you Feel
[1] James 3:5-10
[2] 1 John 1:8
[3] Proverbs 21:2
[4] Romans 1:19-20
[5] Proverbs 14:12
[6] Jeremiah 2:22
[7] Romans 1:22-27
[8] Romans 8:22-25
[9] Mark 2:16-17
[10] Acts 4:10-12

The Gospel and your Gender
[1] Galatians 2:21
[2] Romans 3:19-20
[3] Luke 18:9-14
[4] 1 Corinthians 15:1-7
[5] Galatians 5:1-6
[6] Ephesians 2:8-9
[7] Romans 6:15-18
[8] 2 Corinthians 5:14-15
[9] Colossians 1:9-10

Acknowledgements

No book comes together without the help of many people. I would like to acknowledge those who have contributed to the completion of this work.

I thank my wife for her patience and steadfast love. This project kept me busy for many late nights and early mornings. Ashley, you are my partner in ministry, and I love you. Thank you for taking the time to help me write the chapter on marriage.

I thank Brooke, Matt, Sean, Steve and Shanen for opening up their lives and writing about their personal life experiences.

I thank Kyle Ferguson for doing a full edit of the book. Thank you for your careful reading of the first manuscript. Your theological insights were very helpful.

I thank Whitney Pipkin for her professional editing prowess. Your recommendation on how to best organize the content of this book was spot on. You have a way with words. Thank you for putting your professional skill to work for the glory of God.

I thank Sean McCoskey for his creative mind and the development of the cover design.

I thank Nathan Hall for taking the long trip to Wichita and putting together a solid video for the project. Thank you for giving away your time and your talents.

I thank the Acts 29 network for their insistence on planting churches that honor God and love people. I count it a blessing to be a member of such a talented network of church planters and pastors.

I thank The Seed Church where I have the privilege of pastoring some of the most valiant men and valued women I know. Thank you for making it possible for me to write this book. I love being your pastor.

Most of all, I thank God for calling me to preach His Word and to pastor His people. Any benefit this book brings to anyone is a testament to God's redemptive power. May this book bring glory to His great name. Amen!